2001

Tanzania at the Turn of the Century

From Reforms to Sustained Growth and Poverty Reduction

Government of the United Republic of Tanzania

The World Bank
Washington, D.C.

World Bank Country Studies are among the many reports originally prepared for internal use as part of the continuing analysis by the Bank of the economic and related conditions of its developing member countries and of its dialogues with the governments. Some of the reports are published in this series with the least possible delay for the use of governments and the academic, business and financial, and development communities. The typescript of this paper therefore has not been prepared in accordance with the procedures appropriate to formal printed texts, and the World Bank accepts no responsibility for errors. Some sources cited in this paper may be informal documents that are not readily available.

ISBN: 0-8213-4941-4
ISSN: 0253-2123

Library of Congress Cataloging-in-Publication Data has been applied for.

CONTENTS

TABLES

FIGURES

ACKNOWLEDGMENTS

The preparation of this Country Economic Memorandum was undertaken jointly between the Government of Tanzania and the World Bank. The task managers, Mr. Benno Ndulu (Lead Specialist, World Bank) and Mr. Charles K. Mutalemwa (Permanent Secretary, Planning Commission, Government of Tanzania), would like to register their appreciation for the support received from a number of individuals and institutions who contributed to the preparation of this memorandum.

Overall guidance for the memorandum was provided by the Technical Team and the Steering Committee formed by the Government of Tanzania. The report was prepared under the general supervision of Messrs. Frederick Kilby, Peter Miovic, James W. Adams, and Ronald Brigish (World Bank), who also provided extensive comments on the various drafts.

The principal author for the *Synthesis of Key Messages* (volume 1) is Mr. B. Ndulu (World Bank). Principal authors of the individual sections in volume 2 are as follows:

- "Recent Macroeconomic Performance"—Mr. P. I. Mpango (University of Dar es Salaam).
- "What Matters Most for Growth?"—Mr. R. J. Utz (World Bank).
- "Combating Poverty, Ignorance, and Disease"—Messrs. L. Rutasitara and H. Mwinyimvua (University of Dar es Salaam).
- "Unleashing the Private Sector's Potential for Tanzania's Development"—Ms. P. Ahuja (World Bank).
- "Pacemakers for Sustainable Growth"—Messrs. R. J. Utz and B. Ndulu (World Bank).
- "Zanzibar's Economic Performance"—Mr. R. Mabele (University of Dar es Salaam).

Background papers and significant contributions to individual chapters were prepared by Ms. S. Dhar and Mr. B. Tarimo (World Bank); Messrs. L. Msongole, A. Mwakapugi, and U. Tenende (Planning Commission); Mr. N. S. Magonya (Vice President's Office); Mr. J. Massawe (Bank of Tanzania); Ms. N. Mbilinyi (consultant); and Mr. H. Semboja (Economic and Social Research Foundation).

Able research assistance was provided by Messrs. E. Mungunasi, G. Kabelwa, and J. Mduma (University of Dar es Salaam). Mr. B. Tarimo and Ms. S. Dhar (World Bank) acted as overall coordinators of the drafting team. Ms. R. Covington, Ms. L. James, and Ms H. Mannoro (World Bank) provided dedicated logistical support in Washington and Dar es Salaam. The final draft of the report was edited by Alice Faintich (consultant) and Ms. S. Dhar (World Bank).

Given the pivotal role of agriculture in the Tanzanian economy, the decision was made early in the preparatory work to publish the background research on this sector as a separate report, *Agriculture in Tanzania since 1986: Follower or Leader of Growth* (June 2000). The main findings are summarized in "Transforming Agriculture into an Engine of Growth and Poverty Reduction" (volume 1). Messrs. C. Delgado and N. Minot (International Food Policy Research Institute) were the principal authors of the June 2000 report. Background papers and significant contributions to individual chapters were made by Ms. J. Bitegeko, Messrs. A. Ngondo, and R. Mlay (Ministry of Agriculture and Cooperatives); Messrs. H. Amani, R. Mabele and W. Maro (University of Dar es Salaam); Mr. E. Wiketye (Institute for Development Management); Mr. R. Mfungahema (formerly of the Planning Commission); and Mr. J. Komba (formerly of the National Bureau of Statistics). Messrs. C. Courbois, O. Mashindano and K. Kazungu provided research assistance.

A draft of the Country Economic Memorandum was discussed at a review meeting held in Dar es Salaam in September 1999, with wide participation from the government, the World Bank, the donor community, the private sector, and academic and research institutions in Tanzania. Messrs. J. B. Raphael and Kibao (Zanzibar Planning Commission), and Ms. V. Leach (United Nations Development Programme/United Nations Development Assistance Framework) provided valuable comments. Peer reviewers for this CEM were Mr. David Bevan, (Oxford University); and Messrs. Enrique Rueda-Sabater, Peter Fallon, William Easterly, and Shantayanan Devarajan (World Bank). In addition, Mr. Alan Gelb, Chief Economist, Africa Region in the World Bank, made comprehensive comments on the entire Volume 1. In addition, the memorandum benefited from a review by the World Bank's Quality Assurance Group.

Finally, we acknowledge gratefully the generous financial support provided by the World Bank for the production of the overall report, and by the governments of Denmark and Sweden for the separate report focusing on agricultural development in Tanzania.

Government Fiscal Year
FY01 = July 1, 2000, to June 30, 2001

Currency Equivalents
Currency Unit: Tanzania Shilling (T Sh)

US$1 = T Sh 802.6 (November 2000)

ACRONYMS AND ABBREVIATIONS

HIV/AIDS	Human Immunodeficiency Virus/Acquired Immune Deficiency Syndrome
FDI	Foreign Direct Investment
f.o.b.	Free on Board
FY	Fiscal Year
GDP	Gross Domestic Product
GNP	Gross National Product
HDI	Human Development Index
HIPC	Heavily Indebted Poor Countries
HIV	Human Immunodeficiency Virus
HRDS	Human Resources Development Survey
ICT	Information and Communication Technology
MTEF	Medium-Term Expenditure Framework
NGO	Nongovernmental Organization
ODA	Official Development Assistance
PER	Public Expenditure Review
R&D	Research and Development
TAS	Tanzania Assistance Strategy
TAZARA	Tanzania-Zambia Railways Authority
TFP	Total Factor Productivity
T Sh	Tanzania Shilling
UNDP	United Nations Development Programme

SUMMARY

Tanzania at the Turn of the Century: From Reforms to Sustained Growth and Poverty Reduction is the successor to the Country Economic Memorandum for Tanzania prepared in 1996 (World Bank 1996). The 1996 memorandum focused on the challenge of reforms and paid particular attention to the impact of reforms on growth, incomes and welfare in Tanzania. The current report draws out lessons from Tanzania's development experience of the past four decades, with emphasis on the period since the last report, and assesses the imperatives for higher sustained growth and better livelihood for its citizens in the future.

The 2000 memorandum is organized in three volumes. Volume 1 contains a synthesis of the main results and key policy messages of in-depth analyses of Tanzania's development presented in volume 2 and a separate companion volume on agriculture (World Bank 2000). Volume 2 reviews and assesses Tanzania's actual growth and poverty reduction performance against its large natural potential and against countries at a comparable stage of development, analyzes the main reasons behind the performance record, and then draws out the strategic and institutional imperatives for exploiting the country's vast potential for sustained growth and reduction of poverty in the long and medium term. The analysis focuses on development of the private sector and its increased role in scaling up overall growth and modernization of the Tanzanian economy. One chapter focuses on the Zanzibar economy and its development, even though Zanzibar is part of the union, because the policy and institutional framework for the island are distinct enough to merit separate attention. Volume 3 contains the statistical appendixes.

Current Status of Tanzania's Development

The memorandum assesses Tanzania's current development status against the country's ambition, since independence, to rid the nation of three archenemies, poverty, ignorance, and disease. Forty years later, the war is far from being won, and Tanzania remains one of the 10 poorest countries in the world, even though it is endowed with a rich natural resource base, has easy geographical access to the international market, has had a peaceful and politically stable environment, and has managed to forge a cohesive national identity around a common language. Measured in domestic prices, real income per head is only about 30 percent higher than at independence. Poverty remains widespread and deep, with half of Tanzanians today living without access to the basic needs of livelihood. Poverty is concentrated in the rural areas, where approximately 70 percent of Tanzanians live, although urban poverty has also grown along with rapid urbanization and urban stagnation. Despite the fact that Tanzania's ranking based on the United Nations Development Programme Human Development Index is relatively better than that of its income level, the country has recently lost significant ground in international ranking.

Structural transformation in Tanzania has been extremely limited, and the achievements relative to expectations have been only marginal. Agriculture still dominates the economy. The share of agriculture in total production (45 percent), exports (75 percent), and employment (80 percent)—although lower than at independence—are higher than in most other developing countries. Tanzania's nondiversified economy hampers flexibility to withstand shocks when they occur.

Over the past four years, the Government of Tanzania intensified macroeconomic policy reforms with the aim of creating a more stable macroeconomic environment. These reforms were pursued with the understanding that such stability was necessary to achieve sustained growth, which is required to reduce the pervasive poverty in the country. As a result, Tanzania has progressed significantly in reestablishing macroeconomic stability. Inflation has fallen from levels in excess of 30 percent in 1995 to the current 6 percent; the exchange rate has remained reasonably stable despite the 15 percent depreciation in 1999; the amount of foreign exchange reserves has climbed from about 6 weeks of merchandise imports in 1995 to the current level of 18 weeks; and the overall fiscal balance, including grants, has had a surplus of between 0.8 percent and 1.2 percent of gross domestic product (GDP) in the past 3 years and is projected to remain in the low range of fiscal deficit, and thus accommodate propoor spending. In the medium term, however, this improvement will need to be grounded in a strong fiscal system to ensure sustained macroeconomic stability.

In parallel with the macroeconomic reforms, the Government of Tanzania also carried out structural reforms focusing on realigning the incentive structure toward increased exports, on using scarce foreign exchange more efficiently, on liberalizing markets for goods and services, and on reducing the involvement of the public sector in commercial activities. A large part of gross economic distortions has been dealt with effectively. Although still fragile and shallow, markets are relatively free, the parastatal sector and the civil service are considerably smaller, and a significant improvement in fiscal discipline has taken place, particularly in enforcing cash budgets. While such improvement must be sustained to instill confidence in investors and other economic agents, more effort is needed to bolster complementary structural policies and institutional structures for sustained growth and broad sharing of the benefits from growth. In a variety of institutional investor surveys, Tanzania scores lowest in the areas of structural policies and institutional quality. If the reforms proposed under the Programmatic Structural Adjustment Credit I are implemented as intended, the openness and liberal character of the economy will be on a solid base.

Main Factors Underlying the Slow Development in Tanzania

The report identifies the main factors behind the slow progress in Tanzania's development to be primarily inadequate capital accumulation and productivity growth, poor support for the transformation of agriculture, disrupted progress in building human capital, and delayed demographic transition. The contribution of physical capital accumulation to growth fluctuated significantly during the past four decades. Gross domestic investment in Tanzania increased from about 13 percent of GDP in 1964 to 30 percent in 1991, and then declined sharply to 18 percent in 1997. The decline was due mainly to a fall in public investment as a result of cutting down overall government spending and privatization. The response of private investment to reform measures has remained weaker than expected and has not compensated for the decline in public investment.

A striking feature of the Tanzanian growth experience is that when one juxtaposes the respective growth trends, investment and growth hardly seem to correlate. This was mirrored by the significant losses in investment productivity during the 1970s and early 1980s. It reduced the economywide rate of return from nearly 30 percent in the early 1970s to nearly 5 percent in the mid-1980s. The economy is only slowly recovering from that loss. Underutilization of capacity and poor investment choices were the main culprits. Actual capital accumulation was also much lower than implied by the investment rates because of the poor choices and incomplete projects affecting economywide returns to the investment. With better and more efficient use of its investment, Tanzania's per capita income in 1998 would have been 30 percent higher than what it actually was.

Poor support for the transformation of agriculture has limited the sector's dominant contribution to growth and poverty reduction. It has also limited progress in agricultural intensification and commercialization. Despite being the backbone of the economy and a source of livelihood for the majority of Tanzanians, agriculture was overtaxed during the control regime, and its revival is still constrained by inadequate public support for productivity growth in the sector and stagnant growth in agrobusiness. One of the reasons for slow intensification of agriculture is constrained access to inputs, credit, and timely advice based on sound research. The private sector has been slow in filling the gaps resulting from the withdrawal of public sector involvement in the delivery of these. The main constraints to commercialization relate to the poor availability of price information, poor infrastructure, undeveloped credit facilities, and weak competition in the markets. Underprovision and the poor condition of the rural road network and inadequate connectivity of this network to the main road arteries limit accessibility to markets and raise costs to producers, suppliers of inputs, and crop marketers. The lack of clearly defined and coordinated strategies among the various government institutions for the development of agriculture, and of rural development more broadly, has constrained the development of a coherent strategy for the transformation of agriculture.

Progress in building human capacity was not sustained in Tanzania. Despite the government's efforts to strengthen human capabilities through increased access to formal education, the contribution of human capital to growth declined from 0.3 percent during the 1960s to 0.1 percent during the 1980s. While Tanzania was successful in expanding access to primary education, high dropout and failure rates at the Primary School Leaving Examination resulted in a high share of the population lacking the necessary skills and knowledge to be able to engage gainfully in a modern economy. Tanzania's attainment rates in secondary and higher education are among the lowest in Sub-Saharan Africa. In fact, the data indicate that the share of Tanzania's population with at least some formal postprimary education had declined from 5 percent at independence to 3.2 percent by 1990. A major cause for low enrollment levels is the relatively high cost of secondary and tertiary education relative to income levels in Tanzania. While 80 percent of poor children and 100 percent of the rich complete grade 1, only 40 percent of the poor complete grade 7, compared with 75 percent of the rich.

The HIV/AIDS pandemic poses a major threat for eroding gains made in human development for the past four decades. The rate of HIV infection is estimated to have reached 8.1 percent in Tanzania. HIV/AIDS is not merely a health problem, but also an economic development problem. It has begun eroding the expected longevity of productive life from the peak of 52 years in 1988 to 48 years currently. It is depleting disproportionately the productive and skilled segment of the population, thereby raising the dependency ratio. The HIV/AIDS pandemic is also increasingly claiming a large share of public resources to care for the terminally ill. For example, it has been recently estimated that it takes resources that could educate nine primary school pupils to take care of one AIDS patient. In addition, families and communities bear much of the cost of taking care of children orphaned by AIDS.

Delayed demographic transition has resulted in an excessive burden on the labor force. At 50 percent, the dependency ratio in Tanzania is too high to support adequate saving levels. In combination with a population growth rate averaging 3 percent over the past four decades, it puts immense pressure on the existing labor force to provide for dependents and undermines progress in living standards. The pressure of rapid expansion of demands on the limited capacity of the economy to support the rapidly increasing livelihood needs is a major drawback to growth and poverty reduction. Tanzania, like the majority of African countries, has not embarked on a demographic transition to lower population growth and attaining a more mature age structure. Higher growth of the economy and education are therefore important elements in the effort to stem rapid growth of the population.

Imperatives for Higher Growth and Poverty Reduction

In looking forward, the memorandum takes as a point of departure Tanzania's intention to build on the strengths of peace, unity, and self-esteem and to break with the past weaknesses, as amply exposed in the *Tanzania Vision 2025* and the reform programs pursued for the last decade and a half. During the reform period, Tanzania has achieved macroeconomic stability, is making steady progress in reorienting its economy to a market-based operation, and creating space for exploiting the large potential of private sector initiative. Much as the payoff from these efforts has still to be fully realized, Tanzania Vision 2025 expresses both hope and determination in ridding the country of poverty, disease, and ignorance. It seeks to do so by achieving high and sustained growth, at an average of 8 percent, and halving abject poverty by 2010 and eliminating it by 2025. Furthermore, Tanzania aims to develop a modern, export-led economy and leap into the category of middle-income country.

Long-Term Strategy for Higher Sustained Growth and Poverty Reduction

Both cross-country experience and the high growth recorded in the 1960s indicate that Tanzania can sustain a 6–7 percent rate of growth by exploiting its natural resource potential, sustaining peace, and staying the course of reforms. It will require maintaining an investment rate of 25 percent (not a difficult task given historical rates achieved in Tanzania) and, even more important, raising investment productivity to levels achieved in the 1960s. To increase Tanzania's growth performance, it is necessary to raise the private investment response and enable efficient business operations. Sustained macroeconomic stability, reduced cost of doing business, fair competition, and privatization constitute the main criteria for achieving these results. Given the small size of the Tanzanian economy, growth will only be sustainable if it is firmly rooted in exploiting the domestic resource base, international competitiveness, and the aggressive pursuit of new export opportunities.

Increases in productivity will only be possible if close attention is paid to the acquisition, adoption, and use of various forms of knowledge, including technical know-how. Foreign direct investment, an appropriate communication and information infrastructure, and an improved level of educational attainment are key elements in facilitating productivity gains through knowledge. In light of Tanzania's low postprimary education attainment, it is imperative that measures be put in place to increase the incentives and returns for undertaking such investments. Given the government's limited capacity, it is wise for it to focus on increased public support in areas where externalities are large, such as primary education and preventive health care. Private sector and community participation in the delivery of postprimary education and health will enable higher levels of attainment and cost-effectiveness.

Structural transformation can be expected to occur alongside accelerated growth. Although the secondary and tertiary sectors (for example, tourism and mining) will likely continue to grow at significantly higher rates than agriculture, this does not imply that growth of these sectors should come at the absolute expense of agriculture or manufacturing. Agriculture will, for the foreseeable future, remain the backbone of the economy, and only a prospering agriculture sector can provide the basis for sustainable poverty reduction and accelerated growth in the other sectors. The memorandum estimates that, to achieve the 6–7 percent overall growth, agriculture should grow at 5 percent annually, a considerable increase from the current 3–4 percent growth rate. The prominence of this sector in overall growth and poverty reduction in Tanzania is underscored by the fact that it dominates income generation and has the highest forward linkages and consumption spin-off effects to the rest of the economy, compared with other sectors. T Sh 1 worth of income generated in agriculture generates a T Sh 1.80 increase in overall GDP, compared with T Sh 1.20 if the same income were generated in light industry. In contrast with the past initiatives, support for the transformation of agriculture should hinge on a cohesive, long-term strategy that targets intensification and commercialization. Apart from more effective research and extension, there will be a need for better rural roads to lower costs of access to markets and inputs, better education to facilitate adoption of improved husbandry, increased private credit to fill gaps left by the collapse of public credit institutions, lower and more transparent taxation, and greater contestability of markets.

The industrial sector similarly remains the backbone of modernization. Despite the massive closure of failed public enterprises, industry has managed to continue posting a growth rate, on average, of 5 percent or more in the past decade, implying that new and surviving firms are growing much faster to more than compensate for failing firms. What is needed is to enhance the skill profile for a modern labor force in order to support the buildup of export competence to break into new markets and withstand global competition in a world increasingly becoming dependent on information technology for productivity growth.

Tanzania's rich-resource endowment offers the opportunity to garner additional growth from more intensive exploitation of its resource base. Exports of nontraditional agricultural commodities, increased activity in the mining sector, and expansion of tourism are three areas that already have registered relatively high growth rates in recent years, but these areas still have substantial potential for additional growth in the near future. It is, however, imperative to take measures that increase the linkages with the rest of the economy.

Low density and poor quality of infrastructure is a critical constraint to market integration and efficiency, given the sparse distribution of economic activity in Tanzania. The resource requirements for developing the needed standards of roads, rail, shipping, telecommunication, and power are immense. Support for improving infrastructure is one area where external assistance can play the most effective role in promoting growth and alleviating poverty in Tanzania. However, unlike in the past, where such support is provided for public investment, it ought to be tied to clear commitments in the budgetary provision for recurrent maintenance costs and should complement a dominant private provision of these services. Most critical in this regard is strengthening the management capability of the government to prioritize road investment and develop an effective maintenance system that pays greater attention to cost-effectiveness.

Medium-Term Strategy for Scaling Up Growth and Reducing Poverty

Finally, the report identifies elements of a medium-term strategy for achieving long-term targets of Tanzania's National Development Vision 2025. These necessarily center on sustainable reduction of the poverty that afflicts half of the country's population. The memorandum identifies four pillars of the strategy for the immediate future: a poverty-reducing growth strategy; a cost-effective and improved system for delivery of better-quality public service; containment of the spread, and management of the impacts, of the HIV/AIDS pandemic; and a governance structure that promotes accountability and social inclusion and that upholds basic rights to a decent livelihood.

The imperatives identified for long-term growth are applicable for the medium-term strategy to raise growth. During the initial phase of scaling up, growth should focus on raising productivity, particularly in agriculture, while benefits from an improved policy environment take root and lead to a higher private investment response in the key sectors identified earlier as pacemakers for growth. To ensure that benefits from higher growth are shared widely, the focus of the strategy will be to expand opportunities for the poor to gainful employment. Higher growth of agriculture, a vibrant informal sector and micro-, small-, and medium-size enterprises are particularly pertinent for such broadly based growth. For the poor, improved access to basic education and primary health services is of highest priority to help bolster their income-earning capabilities.

Building competencies and strengthening accountability for improved public service delivery is an important element of the strategy. Enhanced cost-effectiveness in public service delivery entails three main areas of action: improving strategic prioritization of expenditure, adopting a results orientation as the main approach for monitoring the effectiveness of public spending; and strengthening competencies and institutional capacity for managing public service programs prudently, particularly at the local government level. In this regard, the Tanzania Assistance Strategy and the Medium-Term Expenditure Framework provide the vehicles for setting strategic priorities, budgeting, and monitoring effectiveness. The Public Service Reform Program is the main vehicle for encouraging a results orientation, better incentives, and capacity building in the public service.

Containing the spread and managing the impacts of the HIV/AIDS pandemic is of critical and immediate importance for Tanzania's development. The pandemic is most rampant in the productive, prime age cohort of 15–59. Recent estimates put the loss in potential growth due to the effects of the pandemic in Tanzania at 0.7 percent of GDP annually. The actions identified include adoption of a multisectoral national policy on HIV/AIDS; provision of financial resources for cross-sectoral actions against HIV/AIDS in the context of the Medium-Term Expenditure Framework; strengthening the capacity and increasing resource availability to the National Aids Control Committee and the National Aids Control Program to enable better research, extensive surveillance, and intensive public education campaigns; introduction of public health, HIV/AIDS, and peer education in schools; intensive involvement of the local communities, political leaders, nongovernmental organizations, donors, and religious groups in mass education and campaigns against the epidemic, as well in dealing with the increasing number of orphans; and availability of affordable treatment of the already infected population.

Building a more transparent, accountable, and tolerant governance system is also a key element of the strategy. As Tanzania continues its efforts in building democracy, social inclusion—which is a basis for meaningful participation in the development process by all concerned citizens—will increasingly become a right. The ongoing devolution of responsibilities for managing development to local governments and community organizations, and bringing accountability systems into the public domain augur well for promoting inclusiveness. Sustaining freedom of media and improving the flow of information through better and more effective means of communication constitute key forms of strategic actions to this end. In a corrupt environment, the poor are particularly vulnerable to injustice, as they cannot afford the means for paying off dishonest officials. Apart from dealing with grand corruption, which typically raises the cost of doing business and discourages investment, the country must pay attention to petty corruption in the courts, law enforcement, taxation, education, and health at the local level. The anticorruption strategy will need to scale up attention to this level of corruption.

It can be done, play your part. **What is needed is national resolve to proceed, with increased attention paid to effectiveness in application of resources, and in creating a conducive environment and a space for private initiative.**[1]

---

[1] Taken from an address by President Mwalimu Julius K. Nyerere on the Tanganyika Five-Year Plan and Review of the Plan in May 1964.

OVERVIEW

At independence Tanzania declared war on the nation's three archenemies: poverty, ignorance, and disease. Forty years later the war is far from being won. Looking at Tanzania's development performance since independence, the record should be viewed against the poor initial conditions the country faced, particularly the undeveloped institutional capacity and low levels of human capabilities for development. It provides a background for major challenges ahead in raising the living standards of its citizens and in ridding the nation of the three archenemies.

Where Is Tanzania after Four Decades of Independence?

After four decades of independence, Tanzania remains one of the 10 poorest countries in the world. Measured in domestic prices, real income per head is only about 30 percent higher than at independence. Tanzania's per capita gross national product of US$265 is low and far less than Sub-Saharan Africa and East Asia's averages of US$500 and US$970, respectively. The average gross domestic product (GDP) growth rate has been a low 3. 7 percent for the four decades, while the number of Tanzanians has been increasing on average at 3 percent over the same period. Similarly, for Zanzibar alone the average GDP growth rate has been low, falling to–5.4 percent during the economic crisis years (1976–83), but recovering to 3.7 percent during 1984–94, and to 4.8 percent for 1995–98. What is perhaps more striking is that Tanzania has not been able to sustain relatively high and robust growth of an average of the 6 percent it achieved in its first decade of independence, despite sustaining a reasonably high investment rate (by Sub-Saharan Africa standards) in the following three decades. During this period the average growth decelerated persistently, implying a significant waste of resources the country could hardly afford, and in the process engendering an unsustainable debt overhang, since a significant share of this investment was financed through debt. Although growth has recovered somewhat in the last five years, at an average of 4 percent, it remains too low to make a dent in the pervasive and deep poverty prevalent in the country.

Poverty remains widespread and deep, with half of Tanzanians living under conditions of deprivation. Poverty is concentrated in the rural areas, where approximately 70 percent of Tanzanians live. However, urban poverty has grown with rapid urbanization and a stagnant urban economy. Although Tanzania's ranking based on the Human Development Index is relatively better than that of its income level, the country has recently lost significant ground in international ranking. About half of Tanzanians today cannot acquire the daily consumption necessities of life by international standards, the vital statistics of its population are rather low, and human capabilities for self-sustenance are undeveloped. Average life expectancy, at 48 years, is also low and below Sub-Saharan Africa's average of 52.5 years. The infant mortality rate is 85 per 1,000 live births, and the total fertility rate is 5.5 children per woman. Thirty-two percent of Tanzania's population aged 15 years and above is illiterate. The primary school gross enrollment ratio is officially estimated at 76 percent, but the net enrollment ratio is 56.7 percent. It currently takes an average of 9.4 years instead of the expected 7 years to complete primary education, the extra 2.4 years being due to dropouts and repetition, especially at standard 4 level. In 1996, the secondary school gross enrollment ratio was only 6 percent, far lower than the 27 percent average for Sub-Saharan Africa and 69 percent average for East Asia. This low enrollment ratio is based on six years of secondary education. If the widely used standard of four years of secondary education is adopted, the gross enrollment ratio rises to 9 percent, but is still significantly lower than the African average.

Significant progress has been made in the macroeconomic and structural reform program of the central government. Over the past four years, the Government of Tanzania intensified macroeconomic policy reforms with the aim of creating a more stable macroeconomic environment. These reforms were pursued with the understanding that such stability was necessary to achieve sustained growth, which is required to reduce the pervasive poverty in the country. As a result, Tanzania has progressed significantly in reestablishing macroeconomic stability:

- Inflation has fallen from levels exceeding 30 percent in 1995 to the current 6 percent.
- The exchange rate has remained reasonably stable despite the 15 percent depreciation in 1999.
- The foreign exchange reserves position has climbed from about 6 weeks of merchandise imports in 1995 to the current level of 18 weeks.
- The overall fiscal balance, including grants, has had a surplus of between 0.8 percent and 1.2 percent of GDP in the past three years and is projected to remain in the low range of fiscal deficit, which would accommodate an expansion of propoor spending.

In the medium-term, however, this improvement will need to be grounded in a strong fiscal system to ensure sustained macroeconomic stability.

In parallel with the macroeconomic reforms, the government also carried out structural reforms focusing on realigning the incentive structure toward increased exports, using scarce foreign exchange more efficiently, liberalizing markets for goods and services, and reducing the involvement of the public sector in commercial activities. A large part of gross economic distortions has been dealt with effectively. Although still fragile and shallow, markets are relatively free; the parastatal sector and the civil service are considerably smaller; and a significant improvement in fiscal discipline has taken place, particularly in enforcing cash budgets. While such improvement must be sustained to instill confidence in investors and other economic agents, more effort is needed to bolster complementary structural policies and institutional structures for sustained growth and broad sharing of the benefits from growth. In a variety of institutional investor surveys, Tanzania scores lowest in the areas of structural policies and institutional quality. If the reforms proposed under the Programmatic Structural Adjustment Credit I are implemented as intended, the openness and liberal character of the economy will be on a solid base.

Marginal gains have been achieved in structural transformation. Structural transformation in Tanzania, as elsewhere in East Africa, is extremely limited. The shares of agriculture in total output and employment and of primary exports in total exports have shown the expected downward trend, but remain dominant in total production and exports. Currently agriculture accounts for 45 percent of GDP, which is significantly larger than the expected share for a typical developing economy of Tanzania's size. Over four decades, the share of investment in Tanzania seems to have risen marginally, from 15 percent in the 1960s to an average of 20 percent in the past five years. Comparative structural change indicators for East Africa also indicate that limited structural transformation has occurred in Tanzania. It shows that primary exports as a percentage of exports declined only marginally, from 87 percent in 1965 to 82 percent 22 years later. The corresponding ratio for South Asia declined from 63 to 36 percent over the same period. Similarly, the share of the labor force in agriculture decreased from 90 to 84 percent over the same period. Exports as a percentage of GDP, an important indicator of integration into the world economy, declined from 26 percent in 1965 to 22 percent in 1997. Tanzania's nondiversified economy hampers flexibility to withstand shocks when they occur.

The above situation exists in spite of Tanzania being endowed with a rich natural resource base, having geographically easy access to the international market, having had a peaceful and politically stable environment, and managing to forge a cohesive national identity around a common language. Therefore, relative to expectations, Tanzania to date has not been able to exploit its large potential for growth. The country's lack of persistence in high growth is one of the main factors behind the inability to reduce poverty in a significant way.

What Accounted for the Slow Development in Tanzania?

Inadequate Capital Accumulation and Productivity Growth

The contribution of physical capital accumulation to growth fluctuated significantly during the past four decades. It peaked during the 1970s, when the government introduced a new industrialization strategy and invested heavily in establishing key industries. However, the contribution of these new investments was severely hampered by low productivity, resulting in an overall decline in output per worker, instead of the expected accelerated economic growth. During the 1980s the contribution of capital accumulation to economic growth was only 0.2 percentage points, and declining investment during the 1990s led to a negative contribution of physical capital accumulation to growth.

Although gross domestic investment in Tanzania increased from about 13 percent of GDP in 1964 to 30 percent in 1991, the actual capital accumulation was much lower due to poor choices (white elephants) and incomplete investment affecting economywide returns to these. During the 1990s, the share of capital formation in GDP declined from a peak of about 30 percent in 1991 to only 18 percent in 1997. The decline in investment after 1992 reflects mainly the fall in public investment as a result of cutting down overall government spending and privatization. This memorandum contends that despite declining rates of investment, the higher growth performance in the second half of the 1990s reflects both better choice of investment and higher utilization of installed capacity.

There is a need, however, to expand the productive capacity of the economy for sustenance of long-term growth, and that means increased investment. Private investment, currently at 14 percent of GDP, has not responded quickly to the reform measures undertaken since the late 1980s and has not compensated for the decline in public investment. The overall slow private investment response partly indicates problems of policy credibility. A fragile institutional and policy environment increases the perceived risk to irreversible investment, and hence the adoption of a wait and see attitude by the private sector. The weak response of private investment to economic reforms may also be related to the decline in the volume of complementary public investment (in the form of the provision of basic infrastructure and human and institutional capital), that is necessary for raising the overall absorptive capacity of the economy.

Tanzania suffered huge losses in investment productivity during the 1970s and the early 1980s and is recovering from that loss only slowly. A striking feature of the Tanzanian growth experience that when the rate of growth is juxtaposed with that of the investment rate, investment and growth hardly seem to correlate. The period of the steepest deceleration of growth (1976–84) coincided with that of the highest economywide investment rates. Investment rates averaged nearly 23 percent during 1976–83, when the economy's growth rate decelerated persistently from 6.6 percent in 1976 to –2.4 percent in 1983. The countrywide long-term return to investment declined sharply from nearly 23 percent in 1974 to a low of 4 percent in 1982. During the 1990s the rate of return to investment has climbed up to approximately 20 percent but remains low by the standards of fast-growing economies, for example, East Asia's and Botswana's sustained high investment productivity in excess of 33 percent for more than three decades. Key among the reasons for this tragedy are underutilization of capacity, poor investment choices, and a policy environment that militated against rewarding efficiency. A rough idea of the loss suffered as a consequence of collapse of productivity growth in Tanzania is obtained by looking at the difference between actual and potential GDP. This memorandum shows that, with better and more efficient use of its investment, Tanzania's per capita income in 1998 would have been 30 percent higher than what it actually was. Thus, closing the productivity gap that has opened up since the late 1970s can yield a substantial increase in output based on more efficient use of existing capital.

Poor Support for the Transformation of Agriculture Limited Progress in Intensification and Commercialization

In spite of being the backbone of the economy and a source of livelihood for the majority of Tanzanians, agriculture was overtaxed during the control regime. Its revival is still constrained by inadequate public support for productivity growth in the sector and stagnant growth in the participation by agribusiness. One of the reasons for slow intensification of agriculture is constrained access to inputs, credit, and timely advice based on sound research. Indeed, agricultural research and extension generate high returns on investment, as demonstrated by hundreds of rate of return studies. A study of India indicates that government spending on research and dissemination ranked as the most effective support for raising productivity growth in agriculture. The problems of research and development in Tanzania mainly relate to poor transfer of knowledge from research to application, erratic access to extension agents, and the more recent transitional problems from decentralizing the management of extension services to the local governments. These problems are particularly acute for smallholder crops, such as cotton, coffee, and food crops, in contrast to those such as tea and sisal, where big farmers or marketing and processing companies finance research or provide the bulk of extension services. The use of fertilizer has seen a sharp drop, but this decline has not had much effect on food crop production. Although for food crops the cost-effective use of inputs is a problem, in the case of export crops, fertilizer use is often profitable and probably underused. Better advice and increased input use would help to raise the overall profitability of crop production. Formal credit for agricultural marketing has experienced a spectacular collapse, by two-thirds, in the past five years. As a share of slowly increasing commercial bank lending, loans for agricultural marketing fell from 19.7 percent of the total in 1995 to a mere 0.8 percent in 1999. Just 5 percent of Tanzanian farmers obtain agricultural credit from nonfamily sources in a given year. The main constraint to credit expansion is the perceived high risk of lending associated with poor recovery of credit. The issues faced by the agriculture sector in mainland Tanzania are strikingly similar to those of Zanzibar, including structural characteristics, policy orientation, and contribution to income and employment.

The main constraints to agricultural commercialization are the poor availability of price information, wide marketing margins on account of poor infrastructure, undeveloped private credit facilities, and weak competition in the markets. In 1992 the marketing margins were on average 48 percent of f.o.b. prices for exported crops, and 25 percent for domestic sales, the difference being explained by the longer distances covered to the export points. These margins are still much higher than those in countries in the region with better marketing, much as they have declined significantly in Tanzania since the liberalization of agricultural marketing. Furthermore, there are costs associated with restrictions to crop movements and with excessive taxes and their inconsistent application across local governments. Concerns have been raised also regarding restrictions of access to regional markets in the case of food crops, which hamper the exploitation of profitable market opportunities.

Underprovision of rural road networks and connectivity to the main road arteries limit the accessibility of markets and raise costs to producers, suppliers of inputs, and crop procurers. In the relative effectiveness of different categories of government spending aimed at reducing rural poverty and promoting productivity growth in India, public spending on roads was found to be most effective in reducing poverty largely through raising rural incomes, and it was second only to research and development in raising productivity growth. A similar impact assessment through simulation for Tanzania concluded that low-income, rural farm households that are not oriented toward exporting their crops benefit most from better infrastructure.

The lack of clearly defined and coordinated strategies among the various government institutions responsible for the development of agriculture and rural growth more broadly has constrained the evolution of a coherent strategy for the transformation of agriculture. As a result, actions have tended to be disparate and often reactive in nature. The Ministry of Agriculture and Cooperatives has not been able to galvanize and coordinate the wide range of interventions by the Prime Minister's Office, the Ministry of Regional Administration and Local Government, and the Ministry of Finance with those of its own in supporting the predominantly private sector and nongovernmental organization (NGO) activities in agriculture. The situation is made more complex by the absence of a sectorwide framework and cross-sectoral cohesive strategy, as well as coordination mechanisms for the transformation of agriculture in the context of a rural development strategy. Such mechanisms need to recognize the wide diversity of the needs of the different subsectors, agroclimatic zones, and rural communities. This is a key challenge for transforming agriculture in the immediate future.

Unsustained Progress in Human Capital Development

The contribution of human capital to growth declined from 0.3 percent during the 1960s to 0.1 percent during the 1980s, despite the government's efforts to strengthen human resources and to increase access to formal education. Although progress was made in expanding primary school enrollments, Tanzania's secondary school enrollment ratios are the lowest in Africa, which explains the marginal role education appears to play in raising economic growth in Tanzania. Investment in human capital takes a particularly significant role in a development environment driven by the private sector, as such investment affects the development of entrepreneurial, managerial, and organizational skills, as well as innovation, learning, and adaptation of new technology and modern practices. In addition to contributing to and supporting economic growth, most human-capital investment also directly improves the quality of life of the beneficiaries.

While Tanzania was successful in expanding access to primary education, high dropout and failure rates at the Primary School Leaving Examination result in a high share of the population without the necessary skills and knowledge to be able to engage gainfully in a modern economy. The strong focus of successive governments on enhancing access to primary education is clearly reflected in the sharp decline of the share of the population with no formal education from 80 percent at independence to about 23 percent in 1996. Although entry rates are relatively high (at about 90 percent of the age group), survival rates to the final primary school grade are only 54 percent. The problem is more acute for children from poor and female-headed households. Furthermore, in 1998, 70 percent of primary school pupils failed to achieve a passing grade in the Primary School Leaving Examination. Together with the factors cited above, this implies a relatively low level of human capital formation, despite Tanzania's efforts to achieve universal primary education. Unless measures are taken to reverse it, recent declines in the gross enrollment ratio for primary education further threaten the sustainability of the limited progress made at the primary level over the past 40 years.

With respect to secondary and higher education, Tanzania's attainment rates are among the lowest in Sub-Saharan Africa. The share of the population with at least some formal postprimary education had declined from almost 5 percent at independence to about 3.2 percent by 1990. Postprimary education has clearly not been able to keep pace with the expansion of the population, and even less with the demands of a modern economy. The emigration of skilled labor further accentuates the problem. A major cause for low enrollment levels in postprimary education is the high cost of secondary and tertiary education relative to income levels in Tanzania. The low student-teacher ratio, high overheads (for example, because of boarding and related subsidies disproportionately enjoyed by the better-off), and low utilization of facilities combine to raise unit costs. Only since the middle of the 1980s has access to secondary education expanded more rapidly, mainly through the opening up of the sector to private sector participation.

The HIV/AIDS pandemic poses a major threat for eroding gains made in human development for the past four decades. The rate of HIV infection is estimated to have reached 8.1 percent in Tanzania. HIV/AIDS is not merely a health problem, but also an economic development problem. It has begun eroding the expected longevity of productive life from the peak of 52 years in 1988 to the current 48 years. It is depleting disproportionately the productive and skilled segment of the population, thereby raising the dependency ratio. The pandemic is also increasingly claiming a larger share of public resources to care for the terminally ill. For example, recent estimates indicate that it takes the amount of resources that could educate nine primary school pupils to take care of one AIDS patient. In addition, families and communities bear much of the cost of taking care of children orphaned by AIDS.

Delayed Demographic Transition and the Resulting Excessive Burden on the Labor Force

At 50 percent, Tanzania's dependency ratio is high. In combination with a population growth rate averaging 3 percent over the four decades since independence, the ratio puts immense pressure on the existing labor force to provide for dependents and undermines progress in living standards. The pressure of rapid expansion of demands on the limited means of the economy due to the high population growth in the country and its high dependency structure is a major hindrance to growth and poverty reduction. While in a few countries demographic transition to lower population growth and a more mature age structure has begun, Tanzania, like most African countries, has not embarked on a demographic transition. The problem of rapid population growth in Tanzania remains intact. Population policies and programs for encouraging low fertility (in the demographic sense) sprung up several years ago, but continue to be constrained by limited resources. Higher growth of the economy and education are important elements in the effort to stem rapid growth of the population. The large contribution of population growth inertia to this problem in spite of the actions described above means, however, that for the foreseeable future the country will have to contend with this problem from the side of higher economic growth and productivity to meet growing needs.

Imperatives for Sustained Growth and Poverty Reduction in the 21st Century

In looking forward, the memorandum takes as a point of its departure Tanzania's intention to build on the strengths of peace, unity, and self-esteem; and to break with the past weaknesses. This intention is amply exposed in *Tanzania Vision 2025*, and the reform programs pursued for nearly a decade and a half, albeit with some fluctuation in the first half of the 1990s. Vision 2025 is used in the memorandum both as a statement of hope and to provide a reference point for the country's ambition. The main challenges, identified in this memorandum, relate to long-term economic development and the use of lessons from the past to move forward. At the turn of the century is a good standpoint for a retrospective look and for moving more positively into the future.

Major Features of a Long-Term Strategy for Tanzania's Development

During the last decade and a half, Tanzania has been developing an environment of macroeconomic stability, reorienting its economy to market-based operation and creating space for exploiting the large potential of private sector initiative. Much as the payoff from these efforts has still to be realized in earnest, the *Tanzania Vision 2025* expresses both hope and determination in ridding the country of poverty, disease, and ignorance. It seeks to do so by achieving high sustained growth at an average of 8 percent, halving abject poverty by 2010, and eliminating it by 2025. Furthermore, Tanzania aims to develop a modern export-led economy and leap into the category of middle-income country. Achieving these ambitious targets is undoubtedly a daunting task, judging from Tanzania's past record. This memorandum concludes that the country may still be able to go a long way toward meeting these targets, probably with growth rates closer to the range of 6–7 percent and a more cost-effective strategy for poverty reduction.

Tanzania can achieve 6–7 percent sustained growth—given its natural resource potential, sustained peace and tranquility, and initial low level of income—through a combination of sustaining a conducive policy environment, maintaining an investment rate of 25 percent (not a difficult task given its history), and even more important by raising investment productivity to levels achieved in the 1960s and early 1970s. A more focused and cost-effective delivery of public services will go a long way to raise the economy's absorptive capacity and enable greater efficiency in reducing poverty. Better-quality and lower-cost infrastructure services are key to achieving these targets, and the private sector has a critical role in this regard. The development of an institutional and legal framework supportive of private initiative, similarly, is fundamental for greater efficiency and reduced business risk. Key areas of action in this regard are safeguarding property rights, resolving commercial disputes expeditiously and fairly, creating a level playing field for business through fair competition, and ridding the economy of the high transaction costs associated with corruption.

Further improvement in the policy environment and a market-friendly institutional framework are key to scaling up growth and reducing poverty to a significant extent. The key to significant poverty reduction in Tanzania is accelerated growth. Policy-based projections that take into account recent improvements in the policy and institutional framework indicate that per capita GDP will grow between 1.4 and 1.9 percent annually. Further improvements in the policy and institutional framework raise the predicted annual rate of growth of per capita GDP to the range of 2.4–4.3 percent. Estimates of poverty elasticity indicate that such accelerated growth could lead to a reduction in the share of the population living below the poverty line, from around 50 percent currently to 30 percent by 2015. The effects of HIV/AIDS on per capita GDP growth are difficult to predict with any precision, although the epidemic has already had a huge effect on overall human development. The relatively high incidence of HIV/AIDS has led to a drastic decline in some indicators related to human development and eliminated gains in life expectancy that had been painstakingly achieved during the past four decades.

Achieving the target of accelerated growth will require significant efforts to enhance productivity and increase investment in both human and physical capital. The removal of institutional and policy constraints under the ongoing reforms is an important element in closing the productivity gap between Tanzania and fast-growing economies that has opened up over the past 20 years. As this gap closes, higher rates of growth can be generated from more efficient use of existing capacities. However, further increases in productivity will only be possible if close attention is paid to the acquisition, adoption, and use of various forms of knowledge, including technical know-how. Foreign direct investment, an appropriate communication and information infrastructure, and an improved level of educational attainment are key elements in facilitating productivity gains through knowledge.

Increasing human capital investment requires implementing measures aimed at increasing the incentives for and returns to undertaking such investments, but also increasing public support in areas where externalities are large, such as primary education and preventive health care. Increased public resource allocations to these areas have to be accompanied by increases in the efficiency of service delivery, if the desired increase in the stock of human capital is to be achieved. Furthermore, increased attention needs to be paid to improving the quality of services, as this helps to raise completion rates for primary and other levels of education and increases the use of modern health services. Increased health education would complement the focus on preventive health care in achieving good results. In light of Tanzania's low postprimary educational attainment, it is imperative that measures be put in place to increase the incentives for and returns to undertaking such investments. Given the government's limited capacity, it is wise for it to focus on increased public support in areas where externalities are large, such as primary education and preventive health care. Private sector and community participation in the delivery of postprimary education and health will enable higher levels of attainment and cost-effectiveness.

Investment in physical capital is necessary to sustain high growth rates. One of the key lessons of Tanzania's postindependence experience is the importance of clearly separating areas of public and private investment. The principal source of investment has to be the private sector. However, public investment has an important role to play in providing selected infrastructure services that are complementary to private investments and that are unlikely to be provided by the private sector in sufficient quantities. Another important role for government in this area is providing an appropriate legal and regulatory framework for private sector investment and ensuring property rights and legal contracts. Thus, one of the imperatives for the immediate future is to continue reforms aimed at improving the environment for private sector investment. An area of equal importance is the development of financial markets. At present, financial intermediation is working below expectations. This constrains both the saving rate and the flow of savings to the most productive uses. In addition to domestic savings from both the private and public sectors, foreign savings can also be an important source of finance for domestic investment. While significant resource transfers currently take place in the form of official development assistance, these will need to be supplemented by increased inflows of private capital to finance increased investment levels in the private sector.

Structural transformation, that is, an increase in the share of value added by industry and services with a matching relative decline in the importance of agriculture, can be expected to occur alongside accelerated growth. Although in all likelihood the secondary and tertiary sectors will grow at significantly higher rates than agriculture, this does not imply that this growth should come at the expense of agriculture. Rather, the opposite is true. A potential expansion of manufacturing activities in Tanzania will have to take advantage of various factors specific to Tanzania. These include:

- Easy access to international trade through Tanzania's three sea ports, whose efficiency is being improved through privatization measures.
- A significantly increased, effective power supply from hydro and thermal sources.
- Significant, although not yet fully developed, iron, coal, mineral, and gas deposits.
- Sustained reduction in policy and administrative barriers to trade.
- A stable macroeconomic and political environment.

The main constraints in the medium to long term are likely to be the low level of skills and educational attainment among Tanzania's population and an only rudimentarily developed system of financial intermediation. As progress in these two areas is extremely time consuming, it is imperative that serious efforts to achieve improvements in these areas remain high on the policy agenda and are vigorously pursued.

In spite of the recent emergence of new high-growth sectors, for example, tourism and mining, agriculture will continue to be the backbone of the economy for the foreseeable future. Only a prospering agriculture sector can provide the basis for sustainable poverty reduction and accelerated growth in the other sectors. The prominence of this sector is underscored by the fact that it dominates income generation, is a source of livelihood for 80 percent of Tanzanians, and has the highest forward linkages and consumption spinoff effects to the rest of the economy, compared with other sectors. It is estimated that, to achieve the 6–7 percent overall growth, agriculture should grow at 5 percent annually, a considerable increase from the current 3–4 percent growth rate. Given that poverty in Tanzania is predominantly rural, attacking poverty through growth has to begin in the countryside. Thought needs to be concentrated on transforming agriculture into an engine of growth and poverty reduction. In contrast with the past, a the transformation strategy needs to be made more cohesive by coordinating cross-sectoral interventions and by adopting a policy stance that treats agriculture as a predominantly private sector. Public sector support should be confined to providing a conducive environment for private business and credit, providing better infrastructure, enabling effective research and extension, and sustaining an incentive system that rewards efficiency.

A cohesive, long-term strategy for agriculture-led growth in Tanzania involves at least five central elements: sustaining macroeconomic stability, providing more effective research and extension, improving infrastructure, changing the tax and regulatory environments so that they are more conducive to investment by both enterprises and individual farmers, and developing a coherent institutional framework for a broader transformation of the rural sector. From the evidence presented earlier, what matters most for improved performance of agriculture to a large extent depends on what happens outside the institutions directly responsible for agriculture. While within the sector research and extension have been singled out as most potent for both productivity growth and poverty reduction, better roads and education, increased access to finance, lower and more transparent taxation, and greater contestability of markets are all also critical for success. The question is what is an appropriate institutional arrangement and instruments for pulling these together in a cohesive strategy. A rural development strategy under the Tanzania Assistance Strategy is a useful starting point, and the Medium-Term Expenditure Framework (MTEF) can serve as a coordinating instrument for resource allocation. However, the institutional framework for implementing and monitoring such a strategy will require some reorganization that takes into account the increased involvement of local governments, community organizations, and NGOs within a decentralized approach. It is necessary to design institutional arrangements that can ensure effective intersectoral coordination without at the same time intruding on private sector involvement in agriculture.

The industrial sector remains the backbone of modernization. Despite the massive closure of failed enterprises, industry has managed to continue fostering a growth rate on average of 5 percent in past decade. This implies that new and surviving firms are growing much faster to more than compensate for failing firms. Important lessons have been learned from the disastrous results of overprotecting inefficient firms, from making poor investment choices other involvement by government in enterprise that typically galvanizes a protective regime. This memorandum and another study show that if the reasonable investment productivity of the 1970s had been sustained, industrial growth in Tanzania would have been sustained at 8 percent, leading to a much larger contribution to the economy. The recent stepped-up efforts to privatize industry and dismantle protection augurs well for a more robust development of industry. A new class of entrepreneurs is emerging that does not depend on protective walls and access to subsidized resources. This change in the environment for industrial development needs to be nurtured, albeit against a wave of protectionist lobbies of yesteryear. More fundamentally, however, the skill profile of the labor force needs to be enhanced to bring it up to modern standards. Such enhancement would support the buildup of export competence so that Tanzania could break into markets and withstand global competition in a world increasingly becoming dependent on information technology for productivity growth. Export-led industrialization holds the key to the development of the sector in the future and against the backdrop of a globalizing economy.

Infrastructure is one area where external assistance can play the most effective role in promoting growth and alleviating poverty. Low density and poor quality of infrastructure is a critical constraint to market integration and efficiency, given the sparse distribution of economic activity in Tanzania. The resource requirements for developing the needed standards of roads, rail, shipping, telecommunications, and power are immense. Unlike in the past, where external support is provided for public investment, it ought to be tied to clear commitments in the budgetary provision for recurrent maintenance costs and should complement a dominant private provision of these services. Budget earmarking approaches have been developed through targeting revenue from user charges for maintenance of the infrastructure where public provision is involved. Otherwise, in the case of private provision, a competitive pricing system for all key infrastructure services provides for the financing of maintenance requirements. The establishment and protection of the Road Fund in 1998 was a step in this direction. An independent road agency has now been established. Strengthening the management capability of the government is most critical in prioritizing road investment and in developing an effective maintenance system that pays greater attention to cost-effectiveness. Privatization of the provision of infrastructure services—such as communications, water transport, and power—sets up a basis for lower-cost and more reliable supplies. This in turn contributes to reducing the cost of doing business in Tanzania.

Tanzania's rich resource endowment offers the opportunity to garner additional growth from the more-intensive exploitation of its resource base. Exports of agricultural commodities, increased activity in the mining sector, and expansion of tourism are three areas that already have registered relatively high growth rates in recent years, but which still have substantial potential for additional growth in the near future. However, some of these activities are enclave in character, with only weak linkages to the rest of the economy. This limits their potential to contribute in a significant way to poverty reduction. It is thus imperative to take measures that increase the linkages with the rest of the economy, such as creating incentives for the reinvestment of proceeds from these sectors in other parts of the economy, but also focusing on broadly based development in the private sector rather than making growth depend only on development in these enclave sectors.

Given the small size of the Tanzanian economy, growth will only be sustainable if it is firmly rooted in international competitiveness and the aggressive pursuit of export opportunities. While the strategic pursuit of preferential market access opportunities is also important, these opportunities are bound to become less important with the phasing in of the new World Trade Organization rules and regulations, putting an even greater premium on measures for enhancing international competitiveness. The deepening of regional integration within existing arrangements, such as East African Cooperation and the Southern African Development Community, also has an important role to play in this area. While the enlarging of markets is an important aspect of regional integration, equally important benefits are likely to arise from positive neighborhood effects and spillovers, such as policy and growth spillovers, network externalities from infrastructure, or increased attractiveness
of the region as a manufacturing location for multinational corporations.

Elements of a Medium-Term Strategy toward Achieving the Objectives of the Development Vision

A medium-term strategy for achieving long-term targets of Tanzania's National Development Vision 2025 necessarily centers on sustainable reduction of the poverty that afflicts half of the population. From the beginning, such a strategy should rest on four pillars: a poverty-reducing growth strategy; a cost-effective and improved system for delivery of better-quality public service; containment of the spread, and management of the impacts, of the HIV/AIDS pandemic; and a governance structure that promotes accountability and social inclusion and that upholds basic rights to a decent livelihood.

SCALING UP A GROWTH STRATEGY FOCUSED ON POVERTY REDUCTION. The first action required for poverty reduction is to create an environment conducive to scaling up economic expansion from the current rate of growth of 4–5 percent to 6–7 percent. Second is to ensure that benefits from higher growth are shared widely. Third is to strengthen human capabilities in support of growth and poverty reduction.

37.   Growth will be raised in the medium term through:

- Consolidating and sustaining the recent gains in macroeconomic stability.
- Continuing policy and institutional reforms for building a market-friendly environment.

- Reducing the cost of doing private business (especially infrastructure and burdensome taxation) and creating a capital-friendly environment to harness private sector initiative for a higher contribution to growth.
- Strategically exploiting new opportunities for rapid growth and modernization of the economy through improved performance of the "traditional" productive sectors, that is, agriculture and manufacturing; through sustainable and judicious expansion of some of the newer pacemakers for growth, that is, mining and tourism; and through diversification into new opportunities for rapid growth and modernization, for example, nurturing the nascent information and communication technology service sector.

The initial phase of scaling up growth needs to focus on raising productivity, particularly in agriculture, the dominant sector, while benefits from an improved policy environment take root and lead to a higher private investment response in the key sectors mentioned above. Following successful macroeconomic stabilization, the government should pursue efforts to sustain macroeconomic stability by continuing containment of monetary expansion to noninflationary levels and upholding fiscal discipline to spur a further reduction of inflation to less than 5 percent. Furthermore, the government needs to follow through on its commitments to developing prudent, accountable, and transparent fiscal management; to improve the business environment through making the legal system governing commercial operations more transparent and safeguarding property rights; to reduce the burden from taxation; to provide infrastructure services more efficiently through increasing private sector involvement in transport and utilities; and to develop a procompetition regulatory framework.

To ensure that benefits from higher growth are shared widely, the focus of the strategy must be on expanding opportunities for the poor to obtain gainful employment. Higher growth of agriculture, a vibrant informal sector, and development of small and medium enterprises are particularly pertinent for such broadly based growth. Key to raising agricultural growth are increased productivity; improved access to markets, particularly through improved rural roads; intensification programs with more timely access to advice and more cost-effective input and credit availability; and removal of disincentives to investment and production. The growth of activities under the informal sector and small and medium enterprises can benefit mainly from technological extension services and supportive infrastructure, such as industrial parks and marketing services. At the same time, to maximize employment impacts, efforts should be made to design labor-intensive approaches for rehabilitating and maintaining the rural roads network and to maximize multiplier effects and employment benefits from the growth pacemakers—mining and tourism.

Human capabilities must be strengthened to support growth in a way that increases the capacity of the poor to exploit new opportunities from growth. This memorandum has identified low levels of educational attainment and ill health to be among the major constraints to growth, and the impacts of improvements in these on growth were assessed to be quite significant. Educating mothers has been shown to have a particularly strong effect on increased demand for education by their future offspring (a valuable intergenerational trait), compounding the positive effects of current support to the sector. This view of social service provision goes beyond the traditional view of education and health as welfare measures, to highlight them as key elements of human capabilities for supporting growth. While for the poor improved access to basic education and primary health services is of highest priority to help bolster their income-earning capabilities, overall economywide improvement in skills and knowledge is needed to cope with competition in the rapidly integrating global economy. The ability to absorb and adapt technology, particularly information technology, is of paramount importance for overall productivity enhancement. The nascent efforts in Tanzania for promoting e-commerce and electronic public service offer opportunities to leapfrog technologically into the 21st century. Essential for exploiting this opportunity is strengthening the coverage of secondary education through increasing enrollment rates and improving the quality of teaching, particularly of teaching English, which is the language most widely used in information technology.

BUILDING COMPETENCIES AND STRENGTHENING ACCOUNTABILITY FOR IMPROVED PUBLIC SERVICE DELIVERY. In the last five years, the government has intensified the rationalization of its functions by scaling back its dominant involvement in commercial activities and its virtual monopoly in the provision of social services. Through the privatization program and liberalization of markets, the private sector is increasingly making inroads into what was previously solely public sector activities, including infrastructure. The participation of the private sector in the provision of social services is also increasing. A strategic division of roles seems to be emerging, with the public sector still being dominant in the provision of basic education and primary health, particularly in rural areas, where poverty is most prevalent. As the government rationalizes its functions, greater attention must be paid to the cost-effectiveness of providing higher-quality public services.

Increased cost-effectiveness in the delivery of public services entails three main areas of action: improving strategic prioritization of expenditure, adopting a results orientation as the main monitoring approach for the effectiveness of public spending (value for money); and, strengthening competencies and institutional capacity for managing public service programs prudently, particularly at the level of local government responsible for delivery of essential services. The Tanzania Assistance Strategy and the MTEF provide the vehicles for strategic prioritization, budgeting, and monitoring effectiveness. Tanzania needs to move toward an orientation that focuses on results and away from the traditional approach of accountability on the input side (that is, ascertaining proper use of availed resources). Under the Public Expenditure Review process, preliminary work for the definition of production functions of the various sectors is being carried out, which will enable determination of outputs expected from application of allocated funds. Value for money audits and reviews will ground this approach to impact assessment in a new form of accountability. To enable public servants to deliver services competently and with requisite motivation, there is a need to strengthen personnel and institutional capacity building and to implement pay reform. The operation of the Integrated Financial Management System and timely, as well as comprehensive, audits require professional skills and computer literacy. These improvements are complemented by further rationalizing the functions of governments to a more limited range of activities that cannot be more efficiently supplied by the private sector or that have considerable externalities to the society.

COMBATING THE SPREAD AND MANAGING THE IMPACTS OF THE HIV/AIDS PANDEMIC. The spread of HIV/AIDS is one of the major threats of economic development in Tanzania. The pandemic is most rampant in the prime productive age cohort, the 15–59age group. Relative to what the country could have achieved, HIV/AIDS alone reduced the per capita growth rate of GDP by 0.7 percent per year. Malaria lowered the rate by another 1.5 percent per year. (The malaria morbidity figure for Tanzania is likely to be the highest in Sub-Saharan Africa.) The good news is that the HIV prevalence rate seems to have stabilized in 1994–99. This suggests that prevention activities and information have begun taking effect. The bad news is that the budgetary cost of treatment and basic care is very high. Current estimates show a cost of nearly US$8.9 per capita per year, or US$290 million per year total. Given the low domestic saving rate (3.4 percent in 1996), Tanzania cannot finance the cost of HIV/AIDS on its own, without external assistance. Another important implication for Tanzania is that the HIV/AIDS activities have to be multisectoral. One of the measures in its poverty reduction programs has to be the fight against the spread and impacts of the disease, now designated by the government as one of its top priorities. Comparing Tanzania with other African countries, income inequality is not high, but the access to education is low and decreasing. Education and disbursement of information is crucial in the fight against the spread of the pandemic. The primary education enrollment rate in the country is decreasing, from 85 percent in 1984 to 70 percent in 1990 and 67 percent in 1996. In addition, the secondary enrollment rate is quite low (4–5 percent). Job opportunities for women seem to be among the lowest in Africa, as measured by the female labor force employed in industry. This suggests that gender issues would have to play a central role in HIV/AIDS activities.

A number of actions could be taken to combat the spread and impacts of the HIV/AIDS, including the following:

- Adopting a national policy on HIV/AIDS that cuts across disciplinary and sectoral divides and provides the political and legal framework for an accelerated response.
- Making available financial resources for HIV/AIDS in a planned manner and allocating them through the Public Expenditure Review as guided by the MTEF.
- Strengthening the National Aids Control Program in terms of capacity and resources to be able to do research, surveillance, and wide dissemination of timely reports about the status of HIV/AIDS in the country.
- Intensifying the anti-HIV/AIDS campaigns countrywide.
- Introducing public health, HIV/AIDS, and peer education in schools.
- Ensuring intensive involvement by local communities, political leaders, NGOs, donors, and religious groups in mass education and campaigns against the epidemic, with the objective of reducing the stigma associated with HIV/AIDS by speaking openly about the problem and its reality in people's own professional and personal lives.
- Strengthening the National Aids Control Committee to establish a national body with a clear mandate and the authority to lead a nationwide, multisectoral response to HIV/AIDS with the institutional capacity and resources to fulfill this mandate.
- Ensuring availability of affordable treatment of the already infected population.

BUILDING A MORE TRANSPARENT, ACCOUNTABLE, AND TOLERANT GOVERNANCE SYSTEM. Social inclusiveness is a basis for meaningful participation in the development process by all concerned citizens. It creates space for expression of priorities in development and for eliciting community initiative and unleashing commitment in development programs. As Tanzania continues its efforts in building democracy, social inclusion will increasingly become a right. The ongoing devolution of responsibilities for managing development to local governments and community organizations, and bringing accountability systems into the public domain, augur well for promoting inclusiveness. Sustaining the freedom of media and improving the flow of information through better and more effective means of communication constitute key strategic actions toward this end.

In a corrupt environment the poor are particularly vulnerable to injustice, as they cannot afford the means for paying off dishonest officials. Petty corruption in local administration and taxation, in the judiciary, and in law enforcement are particularly bothersome. Therefore, apart from dealing with grand corruption, which typically raises the cost of doing business and discourages investment, the country must pay attention to petty corruption in the courts, law enforcement, taxation, education, and health at the local level. The anticorruption strategy will need to scale up attention to this level of corruption.

It can be done, play your part. **What is needed is national resolve to proceed, with increased attention paid to effectiveness in application of resources, and in creating a conducive environment and a space for private initiative.[2]**

---

[2] Taken from an address by President Mwalimu Julius K. Nyerere on the Tanganyika Five-Year Plan and Review of the Plan in May 1964.

1. BACKGROUND INFORMATION

The United Republic of Tanzania consists of the area formerly known as Tanganyika, which is now mainland Tanzania; and Zanzibar, which is made up of the islands of Unguja and Pemba. Tanganyika became a sovereign state on December 9, 1961, and a republic the following year. Zanzibar became independent from the United Kingdom on December 19, 1963, and named the People's Republic of Zanzibar after the revolution of January 12, 1964. Tanganyika united with Zanzibar on April 26, 1964, to form the United Republic of Tanganyika and Zanzibar, renamed the United Republic of Tanzania on October 29, 1964.

Geography and Resources

Tanzania is endowed with a rich natural resource base and easy access for international trade. It has a total area of 945,000 square kilometers, of which 883,000 square kilometers are land; 881,000 square kilometers in the mainland and 2,000 square kilometers in Zanzibar. Inland waters occupy 62,000 square kilometers. With about 46 percent of the total land area being arable, the country has a rich potential for agriculture. Tanzania also has a large hydropower potential and a wide range of mineral deposits, including gold, diamonds, tin, iron ore, uranium, phosphates, coal, gemstones, nickel, and natural gas deposits. The terrain of the country varies, as does the climate and agro-ecological zones. The terrain consists of plains along the coast, a plateau in the central area, and highlands in the north and south. The vast majority of the population lives inland, far away from the coastline. The climate varies from tropical along the coast to temperate in the highlands. On average the country gets an annual rainfall of 1,000 millimeters. The wide diversity in the agroclimatic zones minimizes the countrywide risk of weather-related crop failures.

Good land and climate notwithstanding, the country has managed, according to 1993 estimates, to put only 6.7 percent of its land area under cultivation, of which only 1,500 square kilometers is under irrigation and 1 percent is under permanent crops. Of the remaining land area, 40 percent is under permanent pasture, 38 percent is under forests and woodland, and about 15 percent is under other uses. However, this low use rate masks the fact that population densities vary widely, creating pressure on land, especially in the fertile highlands of northern Tanzania and in the cities. Moreover, deforestation and overgrazing threaten desertification of a sizeable proportion of woodlands in the country.

Income and Human Development

Despite its potential and rich resource endowment, Tanzania is among the least industrialized countries in the world. Almost four decades after it became independent, the country has not sufficiently exploited its potential and resources for the benefit of raising the standard of living of its citizens. Real growth has been stagnant, and poverty has remained pervasive and deep. Tanzania's gross national product (GNP) of US$265 per capita is low and far less than Sub-Saharan Africa's and East Asia's averages of US$500 and US$970, respectively. About half of Tanzania's citizens are poor. Average life expectancy, at 48 years, is also low and below the Sub-Saharan Africa average of 52.5 years. Other vital statistics show that the infant mortality rate is 99 per 1,000 live births, and the total fertility rate is 5.5 children per woman.

Thirty-two percent of Tanzania's population aged 15 years and above is illiterate. Although the ratio of gross enrollment (those who enter at level 1 regardless of age) in primary school to the total eligible population is officially estimated at 76 percent, the ratio for net enrollment (those who are enrolled in school at the official school age as defined by the national education system) is 56.7 percent. In Tanzania it takes an average of 9.4 years instead of the expected 7 years to complete primary education, the extra 2.4 years being due to dropouts and repetition, especially at standard 4 level. The gross enrollment ratio in secondary schools is only 5 percent, far lower than the 27 percent average for Sub-Saharan Africa and 69 percent average for East Asia. This low enrollment ratio is based on six years of secondary education. If the widely used standard of four years of secondary education is adopted, the gross enrollment ratio rises to 9 percent, but is still significantly lower than the African average. Table 1.1 presents selected indicators for comparison of Tanzania with selected other countries and regions.

Table 1.1. *Selected International Comparative Indicators, Selected Locations and Years, 1960–97*

Indicator	Period	Tanzania	Kenya	Uganda	Sub-Saharan Africa	East Asia
Income and welfare						
GNP per capita	1997	210	330	320	500	970
Human development index (HDI) ranking	1997	36	46	33	38	88
Rank (per capita income)–rank HDI	1997	21	5	–19	—	—
Infant mortality per 1,000 live births	1960	147	124	133	166	84
	1994	85	70	121	97	17
Population with access to safe water	1990–95	38	53	38	51	93
Daily calorie intake	1992	2,021	2,075	2,161	2,096	3,107
Adult illiteracy 1995						
Male	1995	21	14	26	34	9
Female	1995	43	30	50	53	24
Gross enrollment ratios						
Primary	1980	93	115	50	78	111
	1996	76	85	74	77	118
Secondary	1980	3	20	5	15	43
	1996	5	24	12	27	69
Initial conditions						
Population (millions)	1997	31	28	20	—	—
Growth of population (percent)	1965–97	3.1	3.4	2.9	2.8	1.8
Density per square kilometer	1997	34	47	96	25	108
Land locked	n.a.	No	No	Yes	—	—
Infrastructure						
Paved roads (percent)	1997	4	14	—	16	10
Electric power consumption, 1996 per capita, kilowatt hours	1996	59	126	—	439	624
Telephones per 1,000	1997	3	8	2	16	10
Communications						
Ethno-linguistic index	1960	0.93	0.83	0.9	0.65	—
Newspapers per 1,000	1996	4	9	2	12	—
Radios per 1,000	1996	278	108	123	196	184
Fax machines per 100	1996	—	0.1	0.2	—	0.4

— Not available.
n.a. Not applicable.
Source: World Bank data.

Population

Although on average there is no population pressure on land, delayed demographic transition is holding back development. Tanzania has a total population of about 31 million people, of whom 30.1 million live on the mainland and about 900,000 live in Zanzibar. The crude birth and death rates are 41 and 14 per 1,000 people, respectively. The population of Tanzania has quadrupled over the last five decades, from 7.7 million in 1948 to 31 million in 1998. On the basis of the latest intercensus data, the current population growth rate is estimated at 2.8 percent, implying an annual increase of about 840,000 people per year. Tanzania's population has a higher proportion in the younger age groups than in the older age groups. The proportion of the total population that is under age 15 is about 47 percent, the proportion between 15 and 64 is 49 percent, and the proportion above age 65 is 4 percent. The median age is a low 16.4 years, and the dependency ratio rose from 98 in 1967 to 106 in 1996, indicating a rising and unsustainable burden for adults to fend for the dependent population.

The average population density for mainland Tanzania is 34 people per square kilometer, having increased from 8 people per square kilometer in 1948. This average hides much wider subnational differentials. According to the 1988 census analysis, population density in the different administrative regions ranged from 9.8 people per square kilometer to 976.9 people per square kilometer. Across districts the variation of population density was even wider, ranging from 1.4 people per square kilometer for Babati district in Arusha region to 1,579.4 people per square kilometer for Ilala district in the Dar es Salaam administrative region.

The population of Tanzania is predominantly rural, accounting for 76 percent of the total. The share of the urban population in total, however, has been rising rapidly as a result of a combination of high population growth and migration from rural to urban areas. Census data indicate that the urban population grew from 6 percent in 1967, to 14 percent in 1978, to 21 percent in 1988, and to 24 percent in 1996. Tanzania's rapid urbanization rate is among the highest rates in the world. As a result, considerable pressure is placed on the capacity of urban service amenities and on the growth of opportunities for gainful employment in and around urban centers.

An analysis of the 1978 census showed that 16 percent of the mainland's total population had their birth places outside their regions of residence. This proportion of migrant population varied greatly from one region to another, ranging from 65 percent for Dar es Salaam to 4 percent for Iringa. The population exchange between mainland Tanzania and Zanzibar accounted for only 0.2 percent of the total population. The immigrants to the mainland constituted about 3.2 percent of the total population. The analysis of the 1978 census further noted that, with the exception of Dar es Salaam, most regions that had shown immigration proportions above the national average of 16 percent—Rukwa, Kagera, Pwani, and Tabora—were also high recipients of immigrants. A substantial proportion of the immigrants were either refugees from across the international borders, or peasant farmers who had settled in neighboring regions. In the case of Dar es Salaam, the immigrant population is more heterogeneous in origin.

Labor Force and Employment

Because of the high proportion of young people in Tanzania, the labor force is growing rapidly and outstrips growth in employment opportunities. Fifty percent of the labor force is under 30 years old. The urban labor force is 16.8 percent of the total, and the rural areas host 83.2 percent of the total labor force. The proportion of women in the labor force is 50.2 percent, close to their share in the total population. The rate of growth of the labor force is 3 percent. The number of new entrants into the labor market has been increasing more rapidly than the population growth rate, and the average age of workers has been declining. About 50 percent of the labor force is currently under 30 years old. Tanzania has about 400,000 to 600,000 new job seekers each year (World Bank 1996). The labor force is mostly unskilled and has a low level of education attainment. Only 67 percent of the labor force is functionally literate, 32.1 percent never had any formal education, 21.4 percent went to primary school but never finished, 43.1 percent finished primary education, and 3.2 percent went to secondary school and above.

The statistics given by the Tanzania government (URT 1993) and the World Bank (1996) on unemployment and underemployment differ greatly. Using the same data, the World Bank adopted a rigorous definition of employment status. The unemployment rate ranges between 4 and 10.7 percent, depending on the source of analysis. The Tanzanian government has the total unemployment rate for the population aged 10 years and above at 3.6 percent, with the rate for men at 2.9 percent and for women at 4.2 percent. The government has the overall underemployment rate at 4.1 percent, 4.3 percent for men and 3.9 percent for women. The World Bank reports the unemployment rate at 10.7 percent, with men at 9.2 percent and women at 12.3 percent. According to this source, the underemployment rate is 2.7 percent overall, with men at 2.72 percent and women at 2.68 percent. Underemployment is most prevalent in rural areas, where labor demand declines seasonally.

Sources indicate that employment grew by between 2 and 3.2 percent during the 1980s and 1990s, respectively. The World Bank (1996) reports total employment grew at an annual average rate of 3.2 percent between 1978 and 1988, and continued to grow at the same rate or even faster in the early 1990s. Bol (1995), in contrast, reports employment growing at 2–2.5 percent during the 1980s, with the growth rate slowing to 2 percent in the 1990s. In both cases, the bulk of employment growth was observed to come from traditional agriculture and, increasingly, from the informal sector.

Formal engagement in the civil service, parastatal organizations, and private firms accounts for about 10 percent of the total employment. The Tanzania government estimates that about 0.81 million people are employed in the formal sector as their main activity, of whom about 60 percent are in the public sector (URT 1993). Private sector employment is becoming more important and has been growing at a faster rate of 10 percent. The number of people employed in the formal private sector more than doubled between 1984 and 1991.

More than 80 percent of the employed, working-age population is engaged in agriculture. Most of them work on smallholdings as self-employed or unpaid family workers. Those working primarily as paid employees are few, but involvement in occasional wage work is common, especially for youths, women, and members of lower-income households. More and more family members are refusing to work as unpaid family workers and are instead opting to join the wage-earning employment group of the agriculture sector (Mbilinyi 1993). The informal sector expanded quickly with economic reforms and is considered a growing source of employment, accounting for about 16 percent of the labor force. The Tanzanian government reports that about 1 million people are currently engaged in the informal sector as a main activity, and 1.8 million as a secondary activity (URT 1993). The survey found that one out of four households in mainland Tanzania has at least one person self-employed in the informal sector during the year.

Structure and Potential of Tanzania's Economy

Results from the study by Kenny and Syrquin (1999) indicate that structural transformation in Tanzania, as elsewhere in East Africa, is extremely limited (see table 1.2). The shares of agriculture in total output and employment, and of primary exports in total exports, have shown the expected downward trend but remain dominant in total production and exports. For the past four decades, the share of investment in Tanzania seems to have risen marginally, from 15 percent in the 1960s to an average of 20 percent in the last five years. The share of food consumption in total consumption has likewise remained stagnant at approximately 70 percent of total household expenditure. Comparative structural change indicators for East Africa (Kenny and Syrquin 1999) also indicate that only limited structural transformation has occurred in Tanzania. It shows that primary exports as a percentage of total exports declined only marginally, from 87 percent in 1965 to 82 percent in 1987. The corresponding ratio for South Asia declined from 63 percent to 36 percent over the same period. Similarly, the share of the labor force in agriculture decreased from 90 to 84 percent over the same period. Exports as a percentage of gross domestic product (GDP) also declined, from 26 percent in 1965 to 22 percent in 1997.

Table 1.2. *Structural Change, Selected Locations and Years, 1965–97*

Structural change	Period	Tanzania	Kenya	Uganda	Sub-Saharan Africa	South Asia
Per capita income	1987	180	330	260	330	290
Growth of per capita income	1965–1973	2.0	4.7	0.7	2.9	1.5
	1973–1987	–1.3	0.2	–4.3	–1.4	2.3
	1985–1995	1.0	0.1	2.7	–1.1	2.9
Investment (percentage of GDP)	1965	15	14	11	14	18
	1987	17	25	12	16	22
	1997	20	19	15	18	23
Exports (percentage of GDP)	1965	26	31	26	22	6
	1987	13	21	10	26	8
	1997	22	29	13	32	13
Primary exports (percentage of merchandise exports)	1965	87	94	100	92	63
	1987	82	83	100	86	36
Resource balance (percentage of GNP)	1965	1	1	1	–5	–3
	1995	–38	–6	–9	–3	–3
Value added in manufacturing	1965	8	11	8	9	14
	1987	5	11	5	10	18
	1997	7	10	8	17	19
Value added in agriculture	1965	46	35	52	43	46
	1987	61	31	76	34	31
	1997	47	29	44	18	25
Labor force in agriculture	1965	90	86	91	77	73
	1987	84	81	86	71	68
Urban population (percentage of total population)	1965	5	9	7	14	18
	1987	24	22	10	27	25

Source: World Bank data.

Agriculture and industry are the mainstays of the economy. Tanzania's economy is basically agrarian. The economy depends on agriculture, which is predominantly smallholder and subsistence in nature, marked by backward technology and low use of modern inputs, and has significant linkages to other domestic sectors. Agriculture accounts for about 50 percent of GDP, provides 85 percent of merchandise exports (raw and processed), and is directly or indirectly a source of employment and livelihood for 90 percent of the total work force and the majority of Tanzanians. Industry is dominated by the manufacturing sector, which currently accounts for about 8 percent of GDP and concentrates on agricultural processing and the manufacture of light consumer goods. However, Tanzania has limited production of equipment and machinery. Industrial development has mainly been pursued in the form of import substitution, until recently has been dominated by public enterprises, and is marked by low technological adaptation and absorption. As competition and the privatization of manufacturing enterprises that formerly were publicly owned gather momentum, signs are appearing of gains in efficiency and greater use of new technology. Recently, even as inefficient firms folded and the industrial base shrank, the manufacturing sector has maintained growth rates of between 5 and 8 percent. Both industry and commercial agriculture are considered the main bases for modernizing the economy.

Minerals and tourism are the new pacemakers for growth. Given the natural and mineral endowments of Tanzania, tourism and mining are envisaged to offer a big push toward economic growth. In 1998 tourism contributed 7.6 percent of GDP, up from a paltry 1.5 percent in the early 1990s. The sector's annual growth rate has averaged 22 percent over the past three years. The number of tourists visiting Tanzania has increased by 34 percent, from 360,000 in 1997 to 482,000 in 1998. This increase in tourism boosted foreign exchange earnings from the sector by 45 percent, from US$392 million in 1997 to US$570 million in 1998. Unlike the prereform period, when the sector was dominated by government institutions and lacked a coordinated tourism policy, the core of the tourism business is now market oriented and guided by the National Tourism Policy. As much as 25 percent of the land area in Tanzania has been set aside as wildlife and botanical sanctuaries. The country aims to attract more than 1 million tourists per year by 2010 and raise the tourist sector's contribution to GDP to more than 25 percent. However, for this ambitious target to be realized, more investment will be needed in market research, infrastructure, publicity, promotion, and improvement of service skills.

As regards mining, the opening of the sector to private investment is already showing positive responses, with Tanzania for the past two years being among the top destinations for mineral prospecting investment in the whole of Sub-Saharan Africa, particularly for gold. The government has abolished its monopoly in the sector and adopted the Mineral Policy of Tanzania to guide and spearhead the development of the sector in the market-oriented approach. This response is also expected to help overcome problems of poor technology and widespread smuggling of minerals. Already there are large entries of foreign direct investment (FDI) in the sector, which hitherto was dominated by artisan and small-scale miners, most of whom used crude mining technology and operated informally. In 1998 the mining sector contributed 1.8 percent of GDP and grew 27.4 percent. The target is to raise the contribution by the sector to GDP to 10 percent as new mining operations come on line and a more robust formal market for minerals develops.

Infrastructure remains a key constraint to exploiting Tanzania's potential. To achieve the growth and modernization targets described above, Tanzania must pay closer attention to its infrastructure network to enable improved accessibility to productive locations. The transport network is geared toward serving an economy dependent on the outside world for output markets and imported inputs, leaving gaps for a cohesive network that would help develop the domestic market. The vastness of the country and the wide geographical distribution of its economic activities, partly following the location of natural endowments, have posed enormous pressures on the rather undeveloped communication and transport systems. Statistics show that Tanzania has a road network consisting of only 85,000 kilometers of roads, of which 10,300 kilometers (12 percent) are trunk roads, 24,700 kilometers (29 percent) are regional roads, and 50,000 kilometers (59 percent) are district roads. District roads include 27,550 kilometers of feeder roads, 20,000 kilometers of district-to-district roads, and 2,450 kilometers of urban roads. Out of the total road network, only about 5 percent are paved and 95 percent are unpaved (10 percent are gravel and 85 percent are earth). Of the unpaved roads, only about 14 percent are in good condition, 25 percent are in fair condition, and the remaining 61 percent are in poor condition. The challenge is therefore to upgrade, rehabilitate, and maintain the road network.

The railway system covers about 3,570 kilometers, with Tanzania-Zambia Railways Authority (TAZARA) railway lines covering 970 kilometers and Tanzania Railways Corporation lines covering 2,600 kilometers. Water transport in lakes Tanganyika, Victoria, and Nyasa is not well developed and depends on old vessels. Tanzania has about 123 airports, of which only 11 have paved runways. These include the three international airports in Dar es Salaam, Kilimanjaro, and Zanzibar.

The communication systems, especially the telephone system, are fairly well developed, but have low coverage across the country and are mainly concentrated in urban centers. This shortfall is partly offset by greater use of radios. At 278 radios per 1,000 people, the use of radios in Tanzania is significantly above the Sub-Saharan African average of 196. Television recently has spread fairly rapidly on the basis of private sector initiative but, again, is largely concentrated in the five most important urban centers: Dar es Salaam, Mwanza, Arusha, Dodoma, and Moshi.

Tanzania has not as yet exploited its large potential for power generation. Although its hydroelectric power system is relatively well developed by African standards, the cost of power is relatively high. Cost inefficiencies in the distribution system and low revenue collection are the main sources of the relatively high unit cost of power in the country. The electricity supply is predominantly hydroelectric, with fairly good coverage by the National Grid distribution system, which supplies about 85 percent of total electricity. The remainder of the supply is thermal. A prospective switch from diesel-based to gas-based (using Songo Songo gas reserves) generation of electricity for heating should further lower the overall unit cost of power generation. Currently the power generation capacity stands at 350 megawatts and is set to increase by another 180 megawatts after the commissioning of the Kihansi hydropower project. In 1996 electricity consumption per capita was estimated at 59 kilowatts. However, power service is concentrated in urban centers and rural electrification is still relatively undeveloped. Solar power is not well tapped, and areas with no electricity depend on other sources of power, mainly firewood and charcoal and, to a lesser extent, biogas.

Tanzania is also well endowed with abundant water sources, but the harnessing of this water for irrigation is still inadequate. The installed capacity of water schemes, rated at 1,156,607 cubic meters per day, is still low. Out of this, only about 69.8 percent is fully used. While the overall objective is to provide clean, safe, and adequate water for all by 2002, the current water supply covers only 46 percent of rural areas and about 68 percent of urban centers. Out of the rural coverage, 30 percent is erratic or completely inoperative, while 52 percent of the urban coverage is eroded by technical and commercial losses. In an attempt to improve supply conditions, urban and rural water schemes are being reorganized into autonomous systems. Urban water authorities are aimed at being self-financing, while rural water schemes will still depend on the government budget to a large extent.

Trade is dominated by traditional exports and imports, but is diversifying. Although significant developments in nontraditional exports have occurred in recent years, Tanzania's exports remain dominated by primary agricultural commodities. Seven commodities—coffee, cotton, cashew nuts, cloves, tea, tobacco, and sisal—have traditionally constituted more than half of the value of total exports. Given the still large share of primary commodity exports, Tanzania's export sector remains highly vulnerable to the vagaries of weather and to fluctuations in world market prices. Nontraditional exports that have good potential in Tanzania include manufactured goods, minerals, services (especially tourism), and horticulture. Noncompetitive imports dominated in the past, but competitive imports have increasingly become prominent, creating competitive pressure for more efficient domestic production. This change has brought with it rising cries of protectionism from some local manufacturers.

Institutional reforms focus on supporting a transition to a market economy. Tanzania is governed by its 1977 constitution, as revised in 1984 and 1999. The country is a signatory to the International Human Rights Charter, and its legal system is based on English common law, with judicial review of legislative acts being limited to matters of interpretation. Power is separated into three branches of government: executive, legislative, and judicial. The country is democratic and adopted a multiparty system in 1995. More than a dozen political parties are registered, five of which are represented in the unicameral National Assembly (which governs the union of Tanzania and Zanzibar) and two in Zanzibar's House of Representatives. Elections are held every five years to elect the president and members of the National Assembly of Tanzania and the president and members of the House of Representatives of Zanzibar. The presidents' tenure in office is limited by the constitution to two five-year periods. Politically, Tanzania has been stable. The country owes its stability, in part, to a cohesive national identity that is built around a common language, Swahili, despite the country's multiplicity of ethnic groups. The government recently adopted a decentralized governance structure, but is still predominantly centralized in operation and has weak capacity in terms of public service delivery. To effectively implement market-based economic policies, the government has decided to leave most of the economic activities in the hands of the private sector and concentrate on the core functions of the government. These core functions include law and order, defense and security, the regulatory framework, and the provision of infrastructure.

Over the past four years, the government has embarked on institutionalizing market-oriented economic systems after nearly three decades of a socialist approach to economic and social development. For nearly a decade, economic reforms took place against the backdrop of the inertia of the government's control mentality, as well as property rights and legal systems that were designed to facilitate a socialist economy. This disjuncture accounted partly for the lack of a robust private sector response, as possible reversals were feared. Changes in the perceptions of the credibility of reforms needed to be grounded by binding legal and institutional reforms. Recent public service reforms target changes in attitudes and enhanced efficiency in the delivery of public services. Supportive institutions and changes in the legal provisions are needed to buttress the development of the private sector in the economy and remain the main challenges in enabling the economy to move to a higher level of supply response, growth, and poverty reduction.

2. RECENT MACROECONOMIC PERFORMANCE

Since independence, Tanzania has gone through three phases of strategic development management: from focusing on building national identity, unity, and self esteem; to setting up and later dismantling a controlled economy; and finally to the ongoing process of developing a market economy in place of the control regime. Throughout the four decades the underlying theme was achieving a sustainable exit from ignorance, disease, and abject income poverty (based on private consumption expenditure). In the first phase, the government of President Julius Kambarage Nyerere (1961–85) was mainly concerned with building national unity and self-esteem and an egalitarian society. The focus was on investment, for rapid modernization, and on equitable social development, and much less on macroeconomic stability and efficiency. This approach, while successful in achieving rapid improvement in social welfare, as a result of applying socialist principles and of large external resource inflows, could not be sustained because of weak growth performance. The second-phase government of President Ali Hassan Mwinyi (1985–95) focused on dismantling controls and on introducing a liberal and market-oriented system to rekindle growth. The aggressiveness of changes in the pricing system helped the economy break with the past, entrenched control system. However, it left the foundations of an orderly market system unattended. The current, third-phase government of President Benjamin William Mkapa (from October 1995) has focused attention on sustaining macroeconomic stability, restoring fiscal discipline and creating an institutional base for supporting a transition to a market economy and greater participation by the private sector.

The control model was generally unsuccessful in spurring sustained growth and macroeconomic stability. After the reasonably stable macroeconomic environment of the 1960s, Tanzania experienced nearly two and a half decades of macroeconomic instability characterized by unsustainable resource gaps and low growth. The period of macroeconomic unsteadiness was associated with the preponderance of controls for building and sustaining the socialist model of development, and an import substitution strategy characterized by high protective walls and subsidization of resources. The fiscal regime was supportive of the control model and was closely associated with serving the needs of a patron–client political system. Controls also led to the propagation of a rent-seeking system. The main weakness of the control model was the difficulty in enforcing the system of controls because of a number of exit options. As a result, both the fiscal resource and import capacity bases were eroded, while a parallel economy mushroomed away from official purview and macroeconomic imbalances proliferated.

The initial reform effort for addressing the macroeconomic instability was homegrown and focused on closing resource gaps that emerged in the late 1970s and early 1980s, but was generally unsuccessful in reviving growth. The first intervention was by exhortation under the National Economic Survival Program (during FY81 and FY82), and second, by closing fiscal gaps under the Structural Adjustment Program (during FY83–86).[3] However, distortions in the pricing system were not addressed. Both programs achieved limited success because, in essence, they were not comprehensive enough and the incentive structure continued to militate against revival of exports.

The initial reform effort was followed by a more bold generation of reforms—two economic recovery programs (during FY87–93)—focusing mainly on restoring macroeconomic stability and dismantling the

---

[3] FY means fiscal year.

state-controlled economic setup. In the second program, the government also attempted to deal with the negative consequences of the reform measures on the poor. While the programs succeeded in redressing gross distortions in the pricing system, especially the exchange rate and interest rate regimes, they were not successful in cushioning vulnerable groups from the adjustment costs.

After a two-year hiatus (FY94–95), during which the process of reforms faltered, Tanzania embarked on the current generation of reforms. These focus on making deeper institutional reforms to establish a base for a market-oriented economy by supporting and sustaining market orientation, opening up the political system, liberalizing and developing markets for resources and products (foreign exchange and privatization), and developing institutional capacities, along with a more recent focus on poverty reduction. Notable successes under this generation of reforms include:

- Depoliticizing the pricing system formally by institutionalizing free markets for all resources and products.
- Instituting fiscal discipline through cash budgeting and granting relative autonomy to the central bank.
- Increasing private sector participation in the economy as a dynamo for reviving growth.
- Restoring more orderly aid relations and coordination, with the government gradually moving into the driver's seat.

The key challenge of strategically reducing the pervasive poverty is at an initial stage.

Macroeconomic Stabilization and Growth

Recovery of growth in the second half of the 1990s was robust and mainly driven by successful macroeconomic and structural reforms. Tanzania has maintained a modest but robust average growth rate of 4 percent over this period, as shown in table 2.1. It is now considered the most improved country in Sub-Saharan Africa according to the *Africa Competitiveness Report* (World Economic Forum and Center for International Development 2000) and the World Bank country assessment, which involve a wide range of macroeconomic and institutional indicators. This improvement has received notice by the international press, and Tanzania has been forecasted to be among the top 20 fastest-growing countries in the developing world in the medium term (*The Economist,* December 11, 1999; *Financial Times,* July 24, 2000). Perhaps the most distinct vote for this improvement is by foreign investors who have, over the course of the last four years, increased their investment flows to the country from US$20 million to the current US$165 million annually. This turnaround has been mainly driven by economic reforms aimed at dismantling central state control of economic activities and achieving strong macroeconomic fundamentals.

The analysis presented in this memorandum indicates clearly that the period of macroeconomic instability was associated with a preponderance of economic controls, and poor growth performance. The robustness of recent growth recovery, set against the backdrop of severe weather conditions over the past three years, confirms a clear shift to a higher growth trajectory, most probably reflecting distinctly more benign macroeconomic and structural fundamentals, as well as greater flexibility in responding to shocks. Under the past growth trajectory, similar weather conditions were typically associated with negative real GDP growth rates. The much lower growth performance during 1992–95, when macroeconomic fundamentals severely deteriorated, provides further evidence of the importance of establishing benign macroeconomic fundamentals for growth. An important lesson to be drawn from this experience is that it is necessary and wise for Tanzania to consolidate and sustain the reforms to ensure stable macroeconomic fundamentals that will ensure sustained growth.

Table 2.1. *Tanzania: Macroeconomic Performance Indicators, 1988–98*

Indicator	1988	1989	1990	1991	1992	1993	1994	1995	1996	1997	1998
Real growth of GDP (percent)	4.4	2.6	6.2	2.8	1.8	0.4	1.4	3.6	4.2	3.3	4.0
Real growth of agriculture (percent)	2.2	3.9	5.5	3.6	1.2	3.1	2.1	5.8	3.9	2.4	1.9
Real growth of mining and quarrying (percent)	–1.3	13.0	16.5	11.7	7.7	8.2	15.0	11.7	9.6	17.1	27.4
Real growth of manufacturing (percent)	3.1	5.2	4.1	1.9	–4.0	0.6	–0.2	1.6	4.8	5.0	8.0
Investment (percentage of GDP)	16.5	18.1	26.1	26.3	27.2	25.1	24.6	19.8	16.6	14.9	15.0
Domestic savings (percentage of GDP)	0.8	–2.7	–0.6	–0.6	–2.4	–3.1	–1.2	0.8	5.4	6.2	6.0
Current account deficit (percent of GDP)	11.6	15.5	16.2	19.5	17.4	25.8	17.1	13.3	7.7	8.4	6.5
Money supply (M2) growth (percent)	35.1	28.5	42.1	26.1	38.5	28.8	32.5	26.2	11.6	11.0	11.1
Money supply (M3) growth (percent)	35.1	29.5	43.3	26.9	42.7	39.3	35.5	32.2	8.7	13.3	10.8
Foreign reserves (weeks of imports)	—	—	6.8	8.2	12.4	6.0	9.5	6.6	11.3	16.5	13.4
Revenue (percentage of GDP)	9.9	12.3	12.5	13.5	13.6	10.2	11.4	11.8	13.0	13.4	12.1
Expenditure (percentage of GDP)	15.7	16.1	16.6	15.3	15.3	19.0	17.5	14.1	12.2	12.0	11.1
Fiscal deficit before grants (percentage of GDP)	–5.8	–3.8	–4.2	–1.9	–1.7	–8.8	–6.0	–2.3	0.8	1.1	1.0
Fiscal deficit after grants (percentage of GDP)	–2.4	–0.2	–0.5	0.4	0.9	–5.1	–2.4	1.5	2.2	3.2	1.9
Inflation (percent)	31.8	30.3	35.8	28.7	21.8	24.0	33.5	27.4	21.0	16.1	12.9
Savings deposit rate, average (percent)	21.5	26.0	26.0	26.0	26.0	24.0	25.0	21.1	16.7	15.1	7.0
Lending rate, average (percent)	24.0	26.0	26.0	26.0	30.0	30.0	31.5	35.5	33.5	26.5	26.0
Exchange rate, average, Tanzanian shillings to U.S. dollars	—	—	—	—	—	461.3	521.3	591.6	586.6	612.8	654.1
Exchange rate, average, Tanzanian shillings to U.S. dollars, official	99.3	143.4	195.1	219.2	297.7	405.0	509.6	574.8	580.0	612.1	669.8
Effective real exchange rate index (1990 =100)	79.8	91.0	100.0	89.6	106.5	103.7	102.2	98.0	82.5	73.2	69.4
External debt, debt outstanding and disbursements (percentage of GDP)	167.1	127.9	159.7	150.5	141.5	156.1	178.4	128.7	101.0	90.21	88.11
Domestic debt (percentage of GDP)	—	—	—	—	—	7.2	8.3	12.1	15.6	17.1	17.3
External debt service (percentage of GDP)[a]	10.8	9.6	10.2	8.9	8.5	14.4	15.5	11.2	9.8	6.6	6.3
External debt service (percentage of exports)[a]	83.6	70.8	76.6	70.4	62.2	88.2	61.9	44.8	44.6	36.9	36.4

— Not available.
a. Data are for fiscal years.
Source: Government of Tanzania data.

Despite the success of the recent reforms, growth still remains too low for significant poverty reduction. The encouraging upturn in GDP growth and the economic forecast remain inadequate to have any significant impact on reducing abject poverty. The realized GDP growth is also low compared with the strongly performing economies in the region. This implies that the achievement of higher and sustained growth is imperative for Tanzania in the new millennium. Besides consolidating and sustaining macroeconomic reforms, the focus now should be on achieving sustained and higher growth. Continued lowering of inflation, consolidating fiscal discipline instituted under the cash budget system, and higher as well as more diversified exports will help set a basis for sustained macroeconomic stability and growth.

The government's anti-inflation stance is paying off in spite of its transitional recessionary costs. The tight monetary and fiscal stance pursued after 1995 has led to a record decline in inflation, from 35.9 percent in 1995 to 6.0 percent in June 2000. If the government maintains its anti-inflation stance, coupled with increasing food production—inflation could be further reduced to below 5 percent, a level consistent with that of Tanzania's principal trading partners—the gains in competitiveness could be sustained without putting pressure on the value of the local currency. Although the monetary authority continues to face the challenge of a rising share of less controllable components of the money supply (deposits denominated in foreign currency and capital flows), it has successfully contained the growth of money supply. The government has also avoided financing budget deficits by borrowing from banks through ensuring that expenditure levels are consistent with available resources.

The cash budgeting system has been the fulcrum of instituting fiscal discipline and, in spite of its limitations for flexible expenditure management, it has been a fair price to pay for long-term gains in growth from macroeconomic stability (see figure 2.1). To provide more flexibility in expenditure management in the future, the government has decided on an orderly relaxation from the monthly exchequer releases and moved to a three-month system for committing expenditures. The government, meanwhile, will need to keep a close watch for slippage in fiscal discipline. The application of sanctions on responsible officers in case of abuse of the more relaxed system of expenditure management will be key to safeguarding the gains from past efforts. A further increase in the revenue collection effort and prudent budget management will reduce pressure on violating the new system.

Figure 2.1. *Revenue, Expenditure, and Fiscal Deficits, 1986–98*

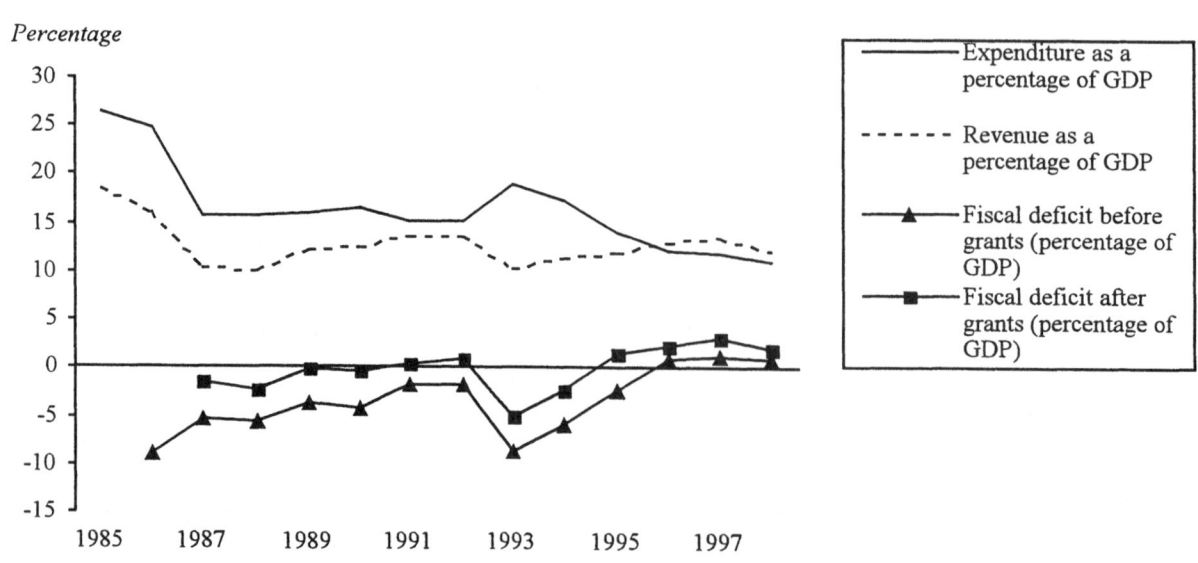

12

Concerns are growing, however, regarding the stringency of the recessionary approach to stabilization (see figure 2.2). This is because fiscal stability has been achieved largely at the expense of compressing public expenditure at a time when public services are deteriorating and key welfare indicators are declining. Over the past three years, budget surpluses have been recorded side-by-side with underfunding of priority sectors. The government has maintained a scheme of reducing the stock of domestic debt to increase resource availability to the private sector, because the private sector has complained about inadequate access to credit. Tanzania has undoubtedly needed to infuse fiscal discipline through cash budgeting and to spur greater efficiency in the delivery of public services. As this prudent behavior takes firm root, the stringency of the recessionary approach to macroeconomic stability needs to be relaxed without compromising the gains in fiscal discipline made to date. Adoption of a medium-term expenditure framework (MTEF) offers the government an avenue for a prudent transition to a less-stringent stabilization strategy, as it enforces the resource-envelope constraint while enabling strategic prioritization in increased spending.

Figure 2.2. *Relationship Between Fiscal Deficit, Government Credit, Money Supply, and Inflation, 1986–98*

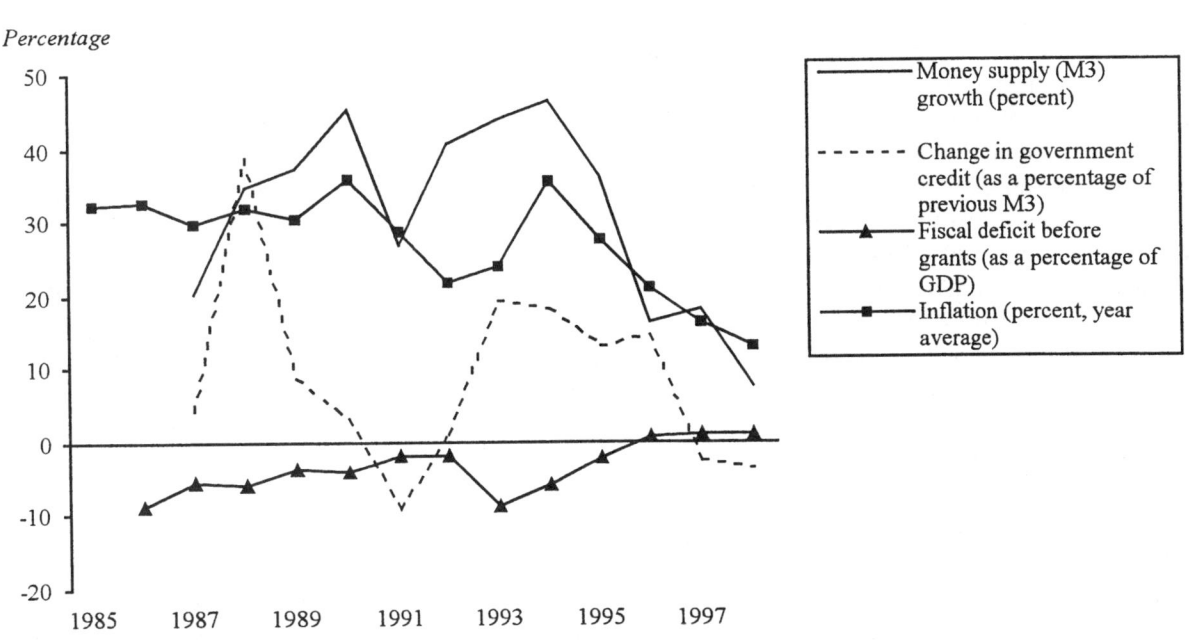

Over the past three years, changes in the Public Expenditure Review (PER) process have enabled significant progress toward strengthening budget management and accountability. Specifically, the predictive value of budgets has been improved through the adoption of the MTEF, enabling strategic prioritization, extension of the coverage of integrating donor finance into the budget frame, and an increased shift of donor finance towards more flexible budget support. The improved PER process has also promoted higher expenditure shares on priority sectors, as well as on maintenance and operations (other charges), the latter and public investment having been treated as a residual in budget allocations in times of tight resource constraints. Budget sustainability is being promoted through continued enforcement of the overall budget discipline through measures for widening the tax net and its revenue buoyancy in the future, and through avoiding recourse to soft financing options, including monetary expansion.

Several measures are now being taken to strengthen the institutional framework for improved fiscal management. To strengthen government accounting and financial reporting, the government has adopted the Integrated Financial Management System in all ministries and has now begun rolling it out to subtreasuries in regions as well as to the districts. The adoption of performance budgeting in all ministries is aimed at developing an orientation toward results in public service delivery. This approach is further strengthened by the adoption of performance improvement plans under the Public Service Reform Program. The Financial Management and Public Audit Acts (2000) have been enacted to replace the old Exchequer Ordinance. The main objective is to grant greater autonomy to the Office of the Controller and Auditor General in carrying out its functions, thus strengthening the public audit system. A key target in the Office of the Controller and Auditor General's future program is to strengthen its capacity to carry out timely audits, particularly those that assess "value for money." As part of a strategy to strengthen effectiveness in the delivery of public services, the government has begun to implement a decentralization program in the delivery of essential services. The Local Government Reform Program grants the primary responsibility for the delivery of basic education, primary health, rural roads, agriculture extension services and rural water to local authorities to improve responsiveness to local demands (citizen's voice) and greater accountability to stakeholders.

Tanzania has been one of the largest beneficiaries of official development assistance (ODA) among poor countries. As a share of GDP, net ODA has averaged about 10 percent over the past five years. ODA also accounts for 58 percent of the total budget and about 25 percent of the public investment. The major concern however, is that 70 percent of the estimated annual US$1 billion worth of ODA is provided outside the budget. Significant progress is now being made through the Tanzania Assistance Strategy (TAS) initiative to develop a framework for integrating ODA into the government's strategic prioritization and improved modalities for partnership with donors. The government and donors are in the process of agreeing not only on priorities but also on the need to strengthen donor coordination to improve the efficiency and effectiveness of development assistance and thus minimize the burden on the limited management capacity in the public sector. Enhanced focus is being placed on capacity building and improving incentives for professionalizing the public service. Under the TAS, avoiding the fragmentation of aid-funded projects and parallel and duplicative donor processes has also been agreed upon. A decision has recently been reached between the government and donors to appoint an independent monitor to assess progress in compliance with mutually agreed-upon measures to improve the effectiveness of aid.

Tanzania's high indebtedness is a drag on the delivery of public services and reduction of poverty. Prospective relief arrangements, if judiciously used, are an opportunity for sustainable exit from the debt overhang problem. Between 1986 and 1998, total external debt stock grew by 62.2 percent. The country used 20 percent of its exports and 30 percent of its revenue to service external debt in 1998. The total disbursed debt stock amounted to US$7,312.5 million by the end of June 1999, representing 665 percent of exports of goods and nonfactor services and 100.6 percent of the GDP. If Tanzania were to pay all the outstanding debt arrears and thereafter remain current, the implied debt-service ratio would have been about 27 percent of exports of goods and nonfactor services, compared with the actual ratio of 16.8 percent as of the end of June 1999. Public domestic debt has also grown rapidly during the 1990s and stood at US$1,324.2 million by the end of March 1999. Given its shorter maturity, domestic debt servicing has consumed a substantial part of government revenue, accounting for about 8–15 percent of annual recurrent expenditure for FY96–99.

Although a number of debt reduction initiatives for Tanzania have been implemented—such as rescheduling, cancellation of debt, debt conversion, and the multilateral debt fund—more comprehensive programs need to be put in place. Thus, the inclusion of Tanzania among the first beneficiaries of the enhanced Heavily Indebted Poor Countries (HIPC) Initiative after the Cologne summit and the introduction of support for a poverty reduction budget to replace the multilateral debt fund as HIPC resources come on stream are critical. The current arrangements of targeting debt relief at poverty reduction offers a useful framework for application of the expanded relief under the enhanced HIPC Initiative. Under the enhanced HIPC Initiative, the ratio of debt stock to exports is expected to be reduced to a sustainable level of 150 percent of exports, involving a total nominal value of US$1,176.8 million over a 20-year period. The relief will enable raising propoor budgetary expenditure. Over the next three years, the Poverty Reduction Strategy Paper and the MTEF project an increase in expenditure on basic education, primary health care, rural roads, water, agricultural research and extension, judiciary, and combating HIV/AIDS from 30.8 to 40.3 percent of the total recurrent budget (excluding Consolidated Fund Services) (see figure 2.3). This initiative follows closely on the multilateral debt fund scheme, which targeted relief for servicing multilateral debt to priority spending on social sectors'.

Figure 2.3. *Share of Other Charges for Priority Areas in Total Discretionary Recurrent Expenditures*

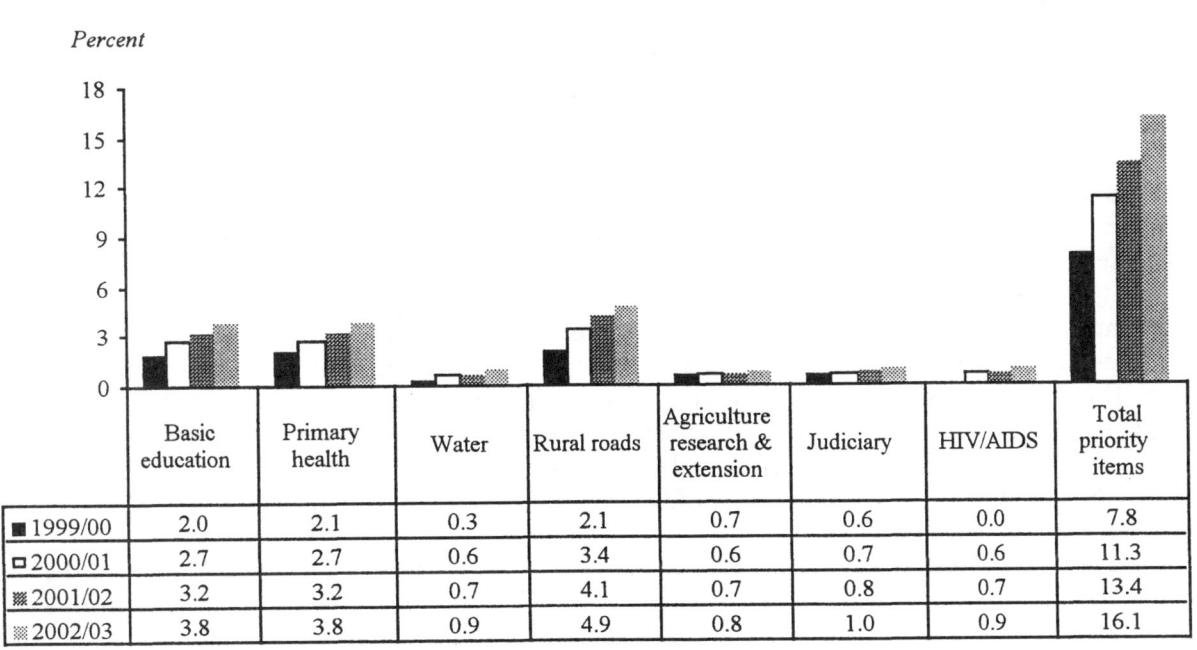

	Basic education	Primary health	Water	Rural roads	Agriculture research & extension	Judiciary	HIV/AIDS	Total priority items
■ 1999/00	2.0	2.1	0.3	2.1	0.7	0.6	0.0	7.8
□ 2000/01	2.7	2.7	0.6	3.4	0.6	0.7	0.6	11.3
▦ 2001/02	3.2	3.2	0.7	4.1	0.7	0.8	0.7	13.4
▦ 2002/03	3.8	3.8	0.9	4.9	0.8	1.0	0.9	16.1

The unfinished agenda of moving toward a robust and sustainable fiscal regime centers around raising the revenue effort through further rationalization of the tax-policy regime and greater efficiency in tax administration. Although Tanzania's tax effort has revived significantly since the reforms collapsed in the first half of the 1990s, with tax revenue growing at an average of 13 percent of GDP over the past five years, it remains below the African average of 15 percent. Unless this problem is addressed, Tanzania will continue to be plagued with the instabilities arising from unsustainable dependence on external aid and continued constraints in financing delivery of public services.

Tanzania's achievement of rationalizing the tax regime and making it more buoyant has been significant. The broad tariff bands have been compressed to the current four positive rates, and income tax rates have been reduced from 11 to 5. The introduction of a value added tax has helped to remove the overall distortionary character of the tax regime and raise its buoyancy. The government has drawn up and begun implementing the agenda for further rationalization of the tax policy. The main problems militating against higher revenue performance revolve around weaknesses in tax administration. Large exemptions and tax evasion constrain the expansion of the tax base and unduly concentrate the tax burden on the current taxpayers. Modernizing tax administration, effectively containing tax evasion and exemptions, and dealing decisively with corruptive practices form the core challenges in improving revenue effort.

Monetary and Financial Policy

The range of interest rate spread widened considerably since liberalization of the financial market, and is now only slowly narrowing. Currently deposit rates range between 5 and 9 percent, while lending rates range between 18 and 22 percent against the backdrop of a 6 percent inflation rate. High real lending rates limit the potential for lowering the cost of finance for investment, while low real deposit rates deter higher financial savings. The good news is that the government has eliminated financial repression by raising interest rates to positive real levels and by allowing free determination of interest rates in the financial market. The bad news is that the margin between deposit and lending rates is wide and expanding. This indicates that competitiveness in the banking sector has yet to be achieved and that perceptions in the banking sector are that interest risks are high. This phenomenon has, among other things, acted to deter savings mobilization and to channel such resources to productive activities. The wide range of interest rates seems to be pointing to the existence of rigidities in the cost structure of the main commercial banks, National Bank of Commerce (1997) Ltd.—or NBC(1997)—and National Microfinance Bank; high credit risks based on past high default rates; and a lack of robust competition in the banking sector. To correct for this problem, the government has now privatized the state-owned NBC(1997) and is in the process of doing the same with the National Microfinance Bank. There is need to further enhance competition among the private banks, and perhaps reexamine the cost implications to banks of the Bank of Tanzania's minimum reserve requirement.

The government should also put loan repayment enforcement mechanisms in place by instituting well-functioning commercial courts, as this would reduce the risks that deter bank lending to all types of customers. The recent decision to support setting up a credit rating bureau will help reduce the cost of screening potential borrowers from the banking system. Competition in the financial sector will also be enhanced by a more vibrant and liquid Dar es Salaam Stock Exchange, which would expand the range of financial assets available to savers and financial investors.

Tanzania has been able to stabilize the nominal exchange rate, but the extent of overvaluation of the real effective exchange rate has tended to rise in recent years. Over the period 1986–94, the exchange rate steeply depreciated to levels consistent with market conditions and with reestablishing external competitiveness. During the past four years, however, the real value of the shilling has risen as the nominal exchange rate remained relatively stable, but with Tanzania's inflation remaining significantly above that of its main trading partners. With 1990 as the base year, the real value of the Tanzanian shilling increased by 30.65 percent by the end of 1998. The appreciation of the real value of the Tanzanian shilling ate into the profitability of exports and lowered relative prices, particularly for cash crops. Although steadily declining, Tanzanian inflation is still above that of its principal trading partners. Furthermore, the value of the shilling in the market was bolstered by significant inflows of foreign private investment, to add to resumption of official aid flows, while the monetary authorities pursued a tight monetary authority to lower inflation. There was a corrective depreciation of the Tanzanian shilling during 1999, when within three months its value against the dollar fell sharply, by nearly 25 percent in nominal terms and 17 percent in real terms.

Tanzania must lower its inflation further to be at par with its trading partners and to develop effective mechanisms for sterilizing the effects of surges in capital flows. However, the government would be making a mistake if it repoliticized the exchange rate by returning to the practice of setting its value. The past record of taking this approach is certainly not attractive. To the extent that monetary authorities have the resource capacity for smoothing exchange rate movements within a reasonable band, they could pursue judicious open-market interventions. The authorities can also look into measures for further

16

enhancing the efficiency of the foreign exchange market by removing the residual capital accounting controls. It is worth noting that in 1999 the Tanzanian shilling depreciated steeply, by 20 percent, eroding virtually all the gains it had made in the past three years toward recouping a significant proportion of the losses to export profitability.

A decline in credit extended to the sectors that are productive is an impediment to growth. The performance of credit growth, particularly credit available to the productive sectors, has not been impressive after liberalization. The ratio of loans to deposits declined consistently, from 141.4 percent in 1990 to 86.1 percent in 1995, and to a still lower 33.8 percent in 1998 (see figure 2.4). Commercial banks also showed increasing risk aversion in lending, giving preference to holding risk-free government paper. This partly reflects high risks in lending, difficulties on the part of commercial banks to assess the credit worth of private borrowers, and problems associated with the handling of commercial disputes. Thus, initiatives by the Bank of Tanzania to establish credit information bureaus and commercial courts are critical.

Figure 2.4. *Lending Rate and Loan/Saving Ratio*

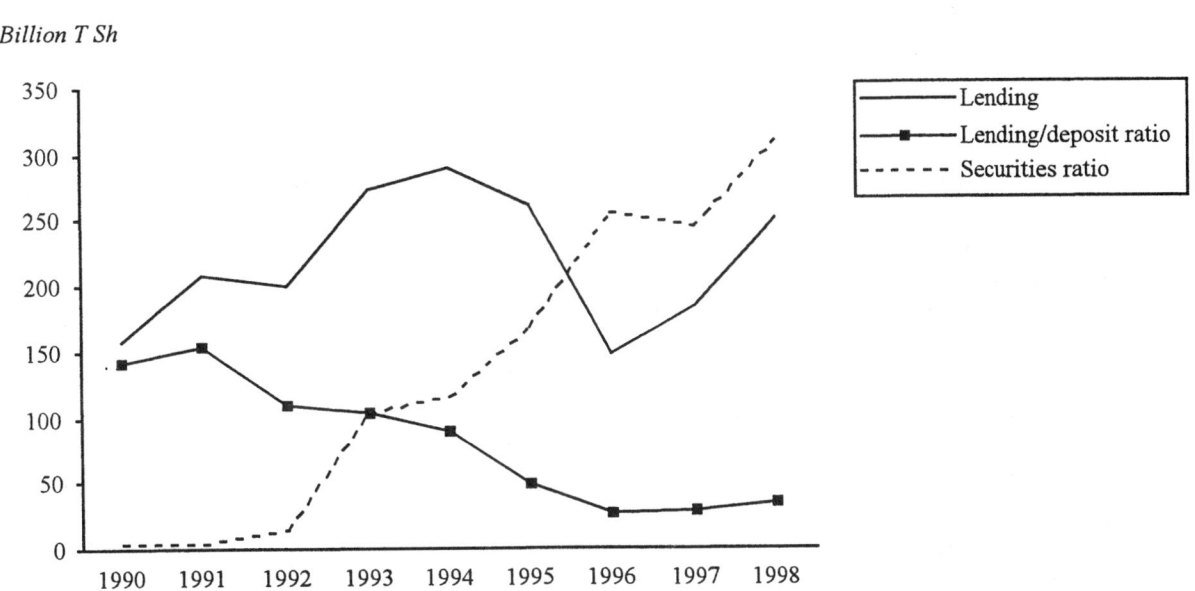

The rural sector is deprived of financial services, and agriculture has experienced the steepest decline in the sectoral share of credit. The collapse of the system that supplies credit for agricultural input and of rural credit schemes has resulted in a significant gap in the provision of rural credit. The concentration of new banks in the main urban centers and closure of remote branches of the National Bank of Commerce has left the gap of financial services to rural areas unfilled. This demands a deliberate strategy to intensify microfinance services and to pursue new initiatives for availing such services.

Managing exogenous pressures on monetary expansion is a significant challenge to the monetary authorities' effort to sustain a low inflation economy. Monetary authorities have to contend with the challenge of holding the lid on the expansion of the money supply in the face of a rising proportion of the money supply being outside of the central bank's effective control. This situation is due to four new main features of the monetary regime. First, interest rates are determined freely in the financial market, so that the Bank of Tanzania can only influence the levels and term structure of interest rates indirectly through changes in reserve money and minimum reserve requirements.

The second feature is the foreign exchange market operating more or less freely with rather insignificant interventions by the Bank of Tanzania, which is limited to smoothening fluctuations in the exchange rate. Autonomous movements in the exchange rates constitute an additional exogenous influence on the valuation of components of the money supply that are denominated by foreign currency, adding to the volatility of the supply.

Third, except for ODA, the management of net foreign assets is no longer under the exclusive control of the Bank of Tanzania. Unpredictable changes in net foreign assets held by commercial banks as well as commercial bank deposits that are denominated in foreign currency, which currently account for about 18 percent of the extended broad money supply (M3), are outside the central bank's direct control. These changes constitute a large, exogenous influence on the money supply.

Fourth, following liberalization of the banking sector, the Bank of Tanzania influences the behavior of banks and nonbank financial institutions mainly through statutory reserve requirements, bank supervision, and moral suasion rather than through the direct control it used before financial sector liberalization. As a result, the effective conduct of monetary policy now depends significantly on the voluntary cooperation of commercial banks beyond the applied statutory measures. This is particularly important as far as the levels of interest rates and expansion of domestic credit are concerned.

Another difficult challenge for the monetary authorities is to be able to prudently reverse the financial disintermediation that set in during the past four years, while avoiding a sharp rise in the liquidity of the economy. Liquidity has declined sharply in the economy during the past four years, as is evident from the sharp decline in the ratios of quasi money and M3 to output, which indicates that the economy is being demonetized. The economy seems to have settled down to a point where it makes do with much less liquidity for the same volume of real economic activity. An important source of this relative liquidity contraction appears to be the slow expansion of credit available to the private sector relative to the extent of retirement of government debt. Another source of contraction is the scaling back of the size of the public sector, which releases resources through the banking system. This liquidity is parked in the banking system, where low ratios of loans to deposits are prevalent. With lending by the National Bank of Commerce and the National Microfinance Bank frozen under a memorandum of understanding with the Ministry of Finance,[4] except for holding treasury bills, excess liquidity in the banking system has risen at a time when the private sector is starved of credit. This characterizes the process of disintermediation referred to above.

As the returns to the treasury bills have now fallen from the giddy heights they attained before 1995 (from an excess of 45 percent to the current range of 8 to 15 percent), commercial banks are hard pressed to look for more profitable outlets. These already have squeezed savings deposit rates as far down as possible to reduce the cost of funds. Thus a strong emission of liquidity from the banking system into the economy is likely to occur as lending activities pick up. To the extent the prospective rise in credit is matched immediately with higher output, inflation will not ensue. However, a transitional period of a lagged output response will probably occur as the gestation period of investment takes its course. This may be a temporary problem, but it needs to be well managed to avoid building up inflationary pressures.

---

[4] Also called the Treasury.

External Trade

Tanzania's export sector remains traditional, with agricultural commodities accounting for about two-thirds of the total merchandise export value. Consequently, a large portion of the export basket is vulnerable to the vagaries of weather and to adverse movements in world commodity prices. Real export earnings declined between 1970 and 1998 because of the decline in the quantity of output (accounting for 70 percent) and because of the terms of trade (accounting for 30 percent). Although rising trends in the export volume have been recorded for all the principal agricultural commodity exports in the past decade, sharp short-term fluctuations in earnings have been experienced, particularly for coffee and cotton. The average contribution of primary exports was 75 percent during 1984–86, before declining to 57 percent in 1996 as the share of nontraditional merchandise exports picked up. Further diversification of the merchandise export base is the single most effective avenue for reducing exposure to economic shocks and for fostering a stable development environment. In terms of foreign exchange earnings, export of services is fast gaining ground on exports of merchandise, mainly through the rapid expansion of tourism. This is an important diversification avenue for foreign exchange earnings.

Tanzania's trade balance has shown signs of improvement recently (see figure 2.5). However, the country still imports more than what it exports by a large margin. Its exports of goods and service finance about 55 percent of its imports. Tanzania's principal imports include mineral fuels, machinery, transport equipment, metals, motor cars, textiles and apparel, food and beverages, and other consumer goods. These are procured from sources that are becoming more diversified, with the share of "other countries" (including African countries) increasing from a range of 17–19 percent to a range of 37–40 percent of the total over the last decade. Tanzania has been a member of various regional blocks, including the Southern Africa Development Community, the Common Market for Eastern and Southern Africa, the Preferential Trade Area, East African Cooperation, and the Kagera Basin and its share of trade with these countries has been rising in recent years. The government has recently embarked on rationalizing its membership in regional and subregional arrangements mainly because of participation-cost considerations.

Figure 2.5. *External Sector Performance*

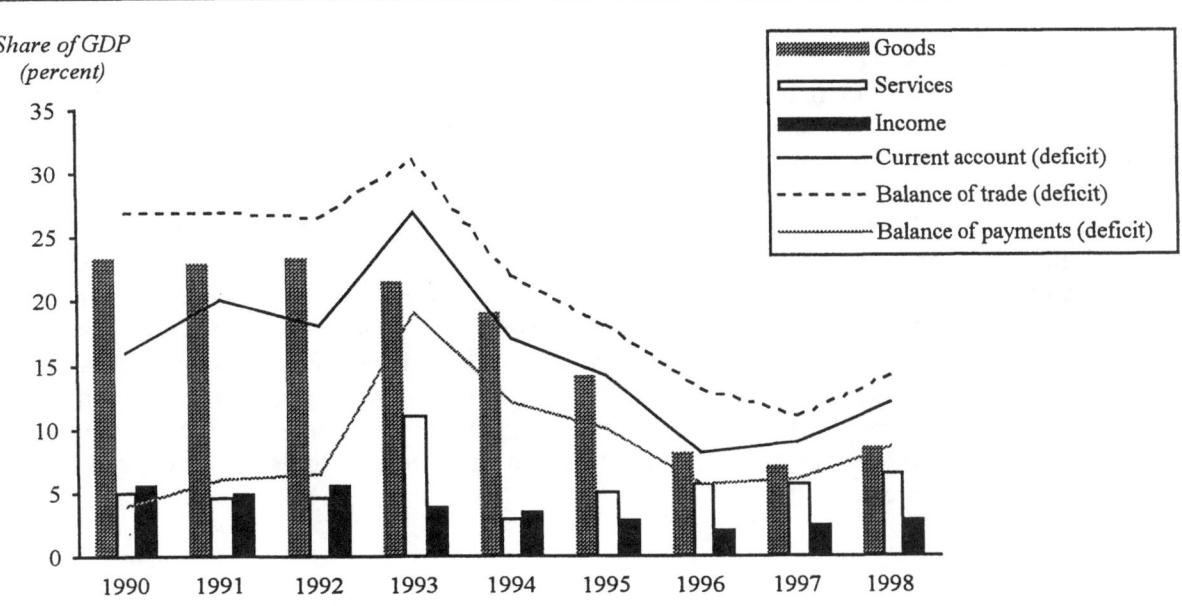

In conclusion, given the already considerable achievement in stabilizing the macroeconomic fundamentals, the focus should now be on five major areas. First is strengthening the fiscal base for sustained macroeconomic stability. Critical to this is strengthening the management of public finance so as to ensure cost-effectiveness in public spending and ultimately reduce excessive dependence on ODA. A key measure is to roll out the application of the Integrated Financial Management System to all ministries and subnational levels of government. The success of the MTEF approach to strategic prioritization of expenditure allocation for effective poverty reduction will depend on the extent of integration of the public financial management, timely availability and transparency of financial reports, and an effective audit system, as well as follow up on recommended actions to deal with the problem of corruption. Also critical is scaling up the revenue effort from the current low level. The Tax Administration Project targets both widening the tax net and improving efficiency in revenue collection. Key among the measures is getting better information on taxpayers, modernizing the tax collection system, improving the transparency and fairness of the tax regime aimed at raising voluntary compliance, and closing revenue leakage through closing down evasion loopholes and taking decisive action against perpetrators.

The second major area to focus on is strengthening the culture of value for money and cost-effectiveness in public service delivery. Pressure on running fiscal deficits can be eased also by higher efficiency in public spending. This approach has not received as much emphasis as mobilization of revenue and external support in Tanzania's past history. The PER process has now begun to focus on outcomes by developing output indicators in relation to input use and introducing performance budgeting. In the medium term, this together with "value for money audits" planned by the controller and auditor general would provide a useful base for complementing longer-term measures for raising revenue and more generally help build a culture of result orientation. Strengthening prudential debt management to avoid the recurrence of unsustainable debt burden will also ensure that available resources would be geared toward spending on essential services.

The third area is pursuing financial deepening and greater competition and thus improving access to reasonable cost credit. Of particular concern here is credit to agriculture. The rural sector is deprived of financial services, and agriculture has experienced the steepest decline in the sector share of credit. Steps must be taken to prudently reverse the financial disintermediation that set in during the past four years in rural areas.

The fourth area is finding ways to raise the efficacy of monetary policy in a context where control over money supply is much more indirect than in the past, which is needed to sustain a low inflation economy. Key to this objective is managing exogenous pressures on monetary expansion caused by large inflows of capital or external assistance and in autonomous movements in the exchange rates.

The final area is implementing prudent management of the exchange rate to avoid eroding the gains in the profitability and competitiveness of Tanzania's exports, which is so crucial for diversification and sustained growth of exports. In this respect there may be concerns about the "Dutch disease" effects from the high growth of mining and tourism sectors, presenting a serious tradeoff with agriculture through possible real appreciation of the Tanzanian shilling. While there are good reasons that this may not happen because a significant proportion of earnings from these two sectors will be externalized to service capital costs and thus provide an avenue for sterilization, in the medium to longer term the authorities will have to find an effective sterilization program to avoid negative consequences on exports more generally and agriculture in particular.

3. WHAT MATTERS MOST FOR GROWTH?

The analysis of Tanzania's performance includes a detailed examination of its GDP growth since independence, over time and compared with other nations, and of sectoral and regional patterns of growth. A close look is also taken at the variability and fluctuations of the economic growth experience in the country. Next, the assessment of the determinants of Tanzania's growth incorporates the relative importance of investment in human and physical capital, and enhancements in factor productivity, to explain its poor growth record. This provides the basis for analyzing underlying factors, such as economic policies, external shocks, and the governance framework, that contributed to low productivity and insufficient—and more important, inefficiently allocated—investments.

Growth Performance

Since independence in 1961, Tanzania's real GDP at domestic prices has grown annually on average by 3.8 percent. With an average annual population growth rate of 3.1 percent between 1962 and 1998, per capita GDP for the country increased only by 0.7 percent. At the end of this period it was only about 30 percent higher than in 1961 (see figure 3.1). If the future growth performance of Tanzania were to be the same as in the past, it would take another 60 years for per capita GDP to double from its level at the time of independence.

Figure 3.1. *Growth Rates of Real GDP at Factor Cost and Population, 1960–98*

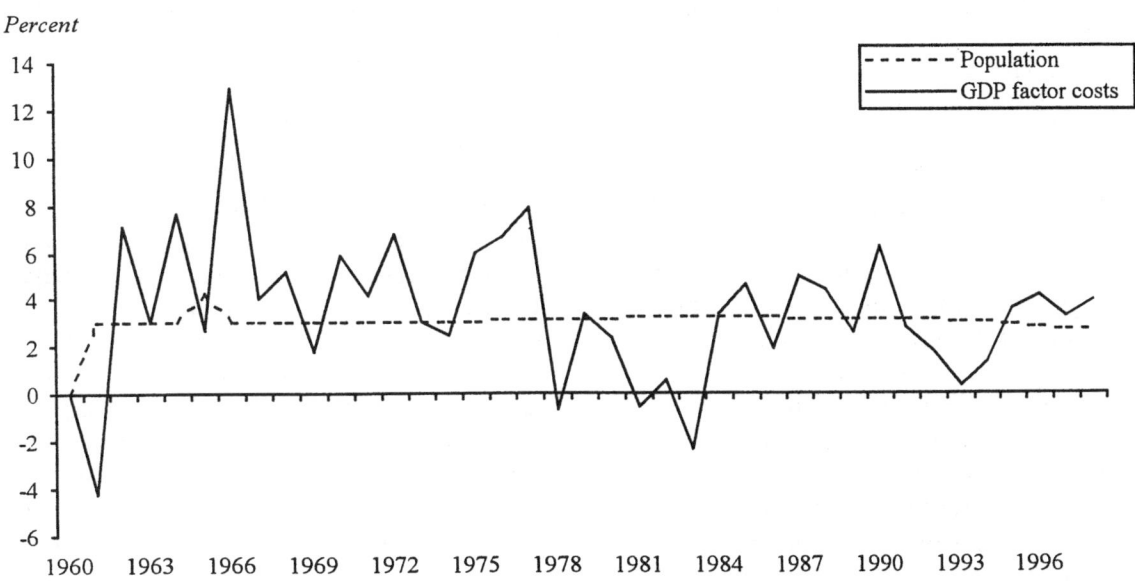

Once economic reforms and liberalization of markets were introduced in Tanzania, the country's economy performed slightly better than that of other market-oriented African economies, while during the years of state control, Tanzania's growth persistently lagged behind. During the first six years after independence, 1961–67, the government pursued market-based policies, with the main objective of increasing per capita income. Growth during these six years averaged 6.2 percent annually. In 1967 Tanzania switched from a market-based system to a policy of socialism and self-reliance. Compared with the preceding years, economic growth slowed down to 5 percent in the 10 years following the Arusha declaration. In comparison, Kenya, which maintained market-based policies throughout, continued to grow at a rate of 7.1 percent during 1968–77, with no apparent change compared with the previous period. In the face of a serious economic crisis during the 1980s, the government adopted a series of reform programs in June 1986. The reform effort included liberalization of trade and of key resource prices and interest rates, dismantling the price control regime, enhancing incentives, and adjusting the exchange rate. Once economic reforms and liberalizing markets were introduced, Tanzania's economy performed slightly better than that of Kenya, while during the years of state control Tanzania's growth persistently lagged behind. Had Tanzania grown at the same rate as Kenya, its GDP per capita would have doubled over the past four decades instead of only increasing by less than 30 percent.

Overall, Tanzania's growth has been slow and halting, with the "golden era" of the 1960s yet to be reattained. In contrast, Botswana's per capita income, which in constant 1985 U.S. dollars was US$535 at its independence compared with Tanzania's US$319, had by 1998 risen to US$2,790 in contrast with Tanzania's US$534. Botswana has maintained a persistently higher growth rate of 4.4 percent for income per capita since independence, while Tanzania's growth rate has averaged a much more modest 1.4 percent over the same period. What are typically regarded as small growth rate differences can make a big difference in the living standards of nations in the long term.

The variability of growth is relatively low. Using the standard deviation of annual growth rates as an indicator, Tanzania shows the lowest variability of growth among 34 African countries for which sufficiently long time-series data are available. One important factor contributing to this decline in variability is the diversification of the economy that took place since independence. With respect to sectoral growth rates, agriculture and finance showed the lowest variability. The relatively small variability of growth rates in the agriculture sector is quite remarkable, given the exposure of the sector to variations in climate and world prices for cash crops. The variability of agricultural growth also declined over the past four decades, reflecting the diversification of the agriculture sector. The mining and quarrying and construction sectors showed the highest variability in growth rates. The variability of growth rates of the manufacturing sector and of public administration and other services was high during the 1970s and 1980s, but relatively low during the 1960s and 1990s. With respect to the manufacturing sector, this high variability reflects Tanzania's changing policy stance toward industrialization, including the problems the country experienced once it adopted a government-led industrialization strategy. The relatively high variability in the growth rate of public administration and other services reflects Tanzania's socialist experiments, which fostered a rapid expansion of the public sector.

Tanzania's dependence on agriculture is high even in comparison with other African economies. In only seven other African countries does agriculture play a greater role than in Tanzania. The Tanzanian economy is dominated by agriculture, which in 1998 contributed 45 percent of value added. In the same year, the service sector contributed 40 percent and industry contributed 15 percent. Agriculture, which has low productivity, influenced overall performance because of its high share in GDP. The trend is, however, changing as growth in other sectors becomes more robust (see table 3.1).

Table 3.1. *Sectoral Growth Contributions, 1962–98*
(*percent*)

	1962–67	*1968–77*	*1978–83*	*1984–90*	*1991–94*	*1995–98*	*1962–98*
Agriculture	2.6	1.3	0.7	1.8	1.2	1.8	1.6
Nonagriculture	3.6	3.6	–0.3	2.5	0.4	2.0	2.3
Industry	1.2	0.8	–0.9	0.9	–0.1	0.8	0.5
Services	2.4	2.9	0.6	1.6	0.5	1.2	1.7
Total	6.2	5.0	0.5	4.3	1.6	3.8	3.8

An examination of the contributions of the agriculture, industry, and service sectors to overall growth shows that during 1962–98, the service sector contributed 2.3 percent to overall growth, agriculture contributed 1.6 percent, and industry contributed 0.5 percent. While the contribution of agriculture to overall GDP growth was fairly stable across subperiods, output growth of the industry and service sectors showed much larger variation. In particular, most of the economic stagnation witnessed during 1978–83 and 1991–94 is attributable to problems in the industry and service sectors rather than in the agriculture sector, although growth in agriculture also slowed down during these two periods.

During the past four decades, the growth rate of monetary GDP was, on average, higher than that of nonmonetary GDP. The difference in growth rates led to a decline in the share of nonmonetary GDP in overall GDP, from 34 percent in 1960 to 27 percent in 1998. This decline implies that the Tanzanian economy is gradually getting out of subsistence. However, this share of nonmonetary GDP is still high.

Per capita incomes in Tanzania vary significantly across regions, but regional disparities have been narrowing. The majority of regions have per capita incomes that are between 10 and 20 percent lower than the national average. These include Mwanza, Singida, Tabora, Mbeya, Lindi, Mtwara, Morogoro, Mara, and the Coastal Region. Kilimanjaro, Dodoma, Kigoma, and Kagera are the regions with the lowest per capita GDPs—between 30 to 35 percent below the national average. Data on nutrition for Kilimanjaro and Kagera also suggest that these regions have the lowest calorific intake. Among developing countries, Tanzania's income inequalities across regions appear to be similar to those observed in many Latin American economies. Within Africa, income distribution across regions appears to be more equal in Tanzania than in South Africa or Kenya. For Tanzania, regional disparities have clearly been narrowing over the past 20 years. Underlying the narrowing dispersion of income across regions are different regional growth rates, but also migration from poorer to higher-income areas. This nevertheless does not take into account transfers from people originating from those regions but residing in other regions.

Explanations for Tanzania's Slow Growth

The analysis of the determinants of Tanzania's growth performance focuses on understanding long-term trends in economic growth and, in particular, on identifying the causes of it's poor growth performance. The analysis is undertaken at three levels. At the first level, the aggregate production function is analyzed using the economic method of growth accounting. This method enables identification of the relative contribution to growth of investments in human and physical capital as well as enhancements of total factor productivity (TFP). In conjunction with this, a closer look is taken at economic policies and institutions, which are key factors determining the incentive regime that drives investment in human and physical capital and factor productivity. At the second level, the analysis focuses on the external environment within which growth takes place, looking at the influence of economic growth of Tanzania's trading partners and neighbors. Finally, the impact of governance systems on economic growth is examined. Governance provides the framework within which economic policies and institutions are designed and shaped.

The most striking aspect of the growth accounting results for Tanzania is the huge decline in TFP between 1960 and 1990. During the first decade after independence, increases in TFP were the driving force underlying economic growth, contributing 1.2 percentage points to an overall annual growth rate per worker of 1.9 percent. In the 1970s, Tanzania experienced a decline in TFP to 0.3 percent, followed by a further decline in the 1980s. During this decade TFP was negative, reducing growth of output per worker by 0.4 percent annually. Underlying the decline in TFP are poor incentives for productivity under a socialist economy; poor macroeconomic policies, which led to foreign exchange shortages and insufficient availability of inputs into the production process; and poor investment decisions by parastatal enterprises, which created capacities that exceeded the economy's absorptive capacity and lacked international competitiveness. The economic reforms initiated in the 1990s brought a reversal to the declining trend of TFP. However, TFP is still low, pointing to the possibility for relatively large gains in TFP growth in the future. Such gains would be both through enhancing the productivity of the existing capital stock and through introducing new technologies, as in countries of East Asia and the industrial countries, which, on average, show significantly higher levels of TFP than Tanzania (see table 3.2).

Table 3.2. *Decomposition of Tanzania's Growth, 1960–98 and Various Subperiods* (*percent*)

Years	Output per worker	Physical capital	Education	Total factor productivity
1960–70	1.9	0.4	0.3	1.2
1970–80	1.3	1.0	0.1	0.3
1980–90	−0.3	0.2	−0.1	−0.4
1990–98	−0.2	−0.2	0.0	0.0
1960–98	0.7	0.4	0.1	0.3

Source: World Bank staff calculations.

The contribution of physical capital accumulation to growth varied significantly in Tanzania during the past four decades. Its contribution to growth peaked during the 1970s, when the government introduced a new industrialization strategy and invested heavily to establish key industries. However, the contribution of these new investments was severely hampered by low productivity, resulting in an overall decline in output per worker, instead of the expected accelerated economic growth. During the 1980s, the contribution of capital accumulation to economic growth was only 0.2 percent. Declining investment during the 1990s in combination with low productivity of investment led to a negative contribution of physical capital accumulation to growth. The contribution of physical capital to growth in Tanzania is below the average for Africa, which is already at the lowest value for all regions.

In many instances, investments were not undertaken at the lowest cost possible. Corruption, lack of government efficiency in undertaking investments, patronage, and a variety of other factors may have led to costs of investment that overstate the actual contribution of investment to capital accumulation. Consequently, the results of growth accounting are likely to overestimate the contribution of capital accumulation to growth and underestimate the contribution of TFP.

The contribution of human capital to growth declined from 0.3 percent during the 1960s to 0.1 percent during the 1980s, despite the government's efforts to strengthen the human resource base and to increase access to education. Furthermore, the contribution of education to output growth in Tanzania is below the African average, and also below the average values of all other regions. Although progress was made in expanding primary school enrollment, Tanzania's secondary school enrollment ratios are the lowest in Africa, which explains the marginal role education appears to play in the determination of economic growth in Tanzania.

The tragedy of slow growth in Tanzania is largely a result of poor productivity growth. A striking feature of the Tanzanian growth experience before the 1990s is that when the growth trend is juxtaposed with the investment rate, periods of high investment spikes and growth hardly correlate. The period of the steepest deceleration of growth (1976–83) happens to coincide with that of historically the highest investment rates. Investment rates (the five-year moving average ratio of fixed capital formation to GDP) averaged nearly 23 percent during 1976–83, when the growth rate decelerated persistently from 6.6 percent in 1976 to 2.4 percent in 1983. This meant that the productivity of investment must have been declining steeply over the same period. The countrywide long-term return to investment declined sharply, from nearly 23 percent in 1974 to a trough of 4 percent in 1982. Similarly, in 1992–94 the growth impact of high investment appears to have been rather weak, even after taking into account the influence of exogenous factors. In contrast, the East Asian countries and Botswana experienced sustained high investment productivity—more than 33 percent—for more than three decades.

Several factors contributed to the investment productivity tragedy. Most important, in the absence of market mechanisms in the private sector and the lack of competition in the political sphere, there were few incentives to use resources well. The prevalence of distortions in policies and markets resulted in poor investment choices and low productivity. This was compounded by a lack of complementary human skills needed to gainfully use more complex capital. During the decade of the deep economic crisis, there was a steep decline in capacity utilization caused by poor investment decisions, import strangulation due to the severe foreign exchange crisis experienced during this period, and poor infrastructure services for operating the installed capacity.

A significant share of investment in Tanzania was financed from ODA. However, aid effectiveness was low. According to United Nations Development Programme (UNDP) estimates, ODA to Tanzania amounts to more than 10 percent of GDP. The share of aid captured in the government budget is, however, only 30 percent, indicating that a significant share of aid bypasses the government budget. Nonetheless, more than 80 percent of the government's development budget is financed through aid. Poor accountability and transparency, as well as a cumbersome implementation mechanism, have led to a situation where many donors prefer to provide assistance directly to local governments, nongovernmental organizations (NGOs), and other beneficiaries. In addition, some aid, such as International Monetary Fund support or support from foreign NGOs, are generally not captured in the budget. In addition to factors such as the adverse macroeconomic and policy environment that affected all types of investment, a number of other factors, described below, led to poor performance of aid-financed investments.

Investment programs often did not take into account the recurrent cost implications of aid-financed investment for ensuring sustainability in Tanzania. Aid-financed investment, coupled with absorptive capacity limitations, leads to capacity expansion without adequate growth of budgetary resources and exports needed to operate or maintain the larger capacity. The problem arose because of the poor integration of aid flows into a government's budgeting and planning mechanisms. Consequently, investment and utilization of ensuing expanded capacity faced two different levels of stringency of resource constraints: a much less stringent constraint on development expenditure financed mostly through aid; and a more stringent constraint on operative requirements (recurrent expenditure), which largely depends on the country's own resources, which are much more scarce. Large aid financing of investment at a time when policy distortions abounded also significantly lowered the cost of scarce capital, hence encouraging the tendency to overinvest relative to absorptive capacity and ignoring the discipline of the appropriate investment choices. A claim can be made that the large flow of project finance in the presence of Tanzania's severe policy distortions was immiserizing to the extent that it cheapened capital and spawned a lack of discipline for judicious choices.

Inadequate attention to the institutional capacity for effective and efficient delivery of public services was one of the greatest constraints to the effectiveness of aid to Tanzania. In the 1970s, a greater emphasis was placed on supporting the expansion of the facilities for social services, particularly under the Basic Needs Program, without sufficient attention being paid to the institutional requirements for more effective delivery of these services. Capacity constraints on project implementation were dealt with by using enclave management units through technical assistance. Efficiency in the delivery of services was underemphasized, with concerns focused instead on ascertaining whether monies were used for their intended purpose rather than on the value obtained from the expended resources. In the earlier years, civil service reforms were driven by the primary objective of downsizing the government to reduce the fiscal deficit. Only recently has attention been turned toward strengthening the government's capability and efficiency in delivering public services effectively. Apart from capacity-building initiatives, these efforts have also begun to address the low motivation of the civil service and its ability to attract and retain high-caliber personnel.

Until recently, accountability systems were fragmented and revolved around a dialogue between the Government of Tanzania and the multitude of donors. The emphasis has been more on externally restraining imprudent behavior by the main intermediary of aid—the government—and not on internal mechanisms for restraint. This arrangement was consistent with the prevalence of autocracy, but is now facing serious challenges as open politics and inclusiveness in the system of governance are being widely adopted, as are anticorruption initiatives by donors as well as by domestic stakeholders. The problem of dual accountability has been recognized, and efforts are being made to resolve it through an integrated approach. The much more sanguine conclusions regarding the ineffectiveness of external conditionality in begetting reform buttresses the shift toward greater reliance on domestic constituencies to motivate and sustain change. This shift also includes promoting the role of the citizens' voice in begetting accountable behavior by those charged with the responsibility for managing the development process.

State capability in the management of the aid regime is critical for promoting growth. Empirical and case studies indicate that aid has had little effect on policy outcomes in Africa, and its contribution to growth has been heavily conditioned by preexisting state capability. It has been suggested that aid was, on balance, undermining institutional capacity in Africa. It has also been suggested that bilateral aid has been an instrument of foreign policy to the extent that important donors tended to support political or ideological clients, rather than the institution of better policy, greater pluralism, or removal of institutional constraints to foster rapid growth. Thus, for the next millennium, it will be critical to strengthen state capability in the management of the aid regime through binding approaches to economic management within a strong institutional and legal framework. Equally important is local ownership of policy and wider participation by local stakeholders in the process of policy formulation and implementation. Donors should implement more selectivity in aid disbursement so as to reward leaders who adopt progrowth policies. Donors should focus their agendas more on policy undertakings deemed to be most potent for growth and poverty reduction.

The country's ability to service its debts was impaired to the extent that the "wasted" investment was financed through debt without corresponding growth returns. Underlying weaknesses militated against gains in productivity growth, as shown in the steep decline in growth in spite of the relatively high investment, and in the lack of factor productivity growth in spite of a drive toward more complex production processes through investment. These were further accentuated by short-run shocks. These factors include poor investment choices, a low skill base for using more complex production technology, inadequate infrastructure, and a poor policy environment. This also links up with the perverse outcome from investment in terms of weak growth effects and the emergence of a severe debt problem since the late 1980s. "Wasted" investment was financed through debt without corresponding growth returns, which impaired the country's ability to service its debt obligations.

The investment rate declined over the 1990s. Gross domestic capital formation increased from about 13 percent of GDP in 1964 to 30 percent in 1991 (see figure 3.2). During the 1990s, the share of capital formation in GDP declined from a peak of about 30 percent in 1991 to only 18 percent in 1997. Most of the increases in the formation of fixed domestic capital that occurred until 1990 were the result of growing private investment. The sharp decline in the investment ratio since 1992 can be attributed to a fall in public investment following privatization and cuts in government development expenditure, while the share of private investment during that period remained relatively stable. However, the fact that, despite the decline in overall investment, economic growth increased, provides a first indication that economic reforms are effective and that investment productivity is increasing. In a rationalized policy environment, investment levels and economic growth are strongly and consistently linked. Thus while initially gains in economic growth can be harvested from the more efficient utilization of existing investment, in the medium to long run the country's ratio of investment to GDP needs to be increased to achieve the economic growth necessary to achieve tangible poverty reduction. Increased investment levels will have to be financed from more zealous mobilization of domestic savings and boosted by continued opening up of the economy to private investment.

Figure 3.2. *Share of Gross Fixed Capital Formation in GDP at Factor Cost, 1964–98*

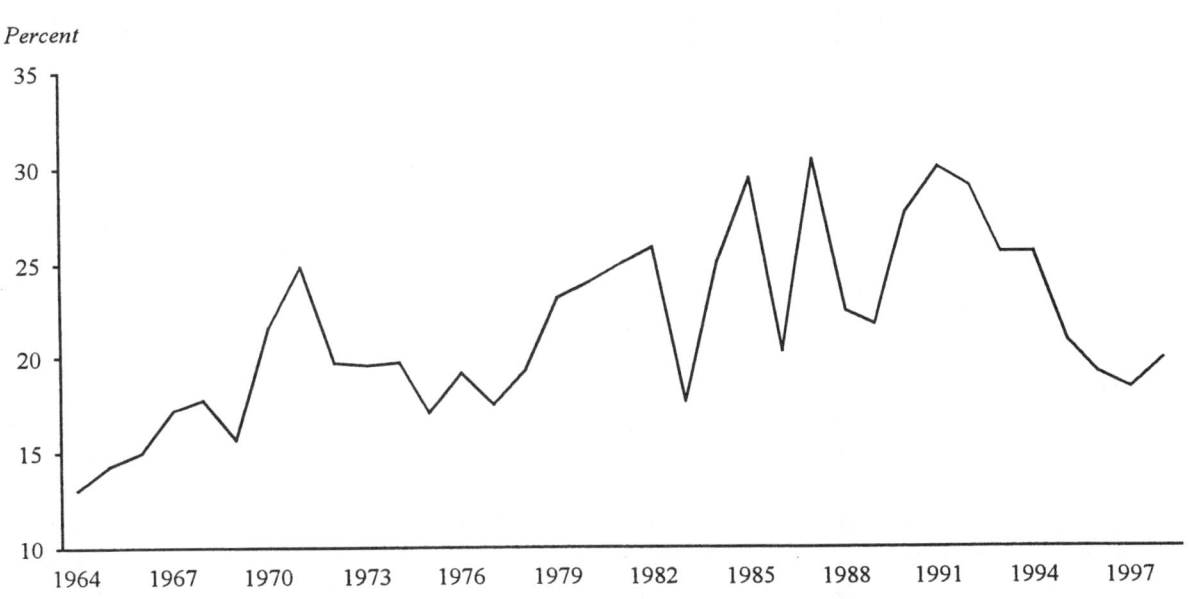

Numerous factors continue to inhibit or scare away investment. Recent performance indicates that, except for mining and quarrying and construction, the private sector investment response to reform measures has been slow. The main reasons include:

27

- A legal framework that functions poorly.
- Administrative and regulatory complexities.
- Poor infrastructure (roads, telecommunications, power, and water supply).
- Inefficient and unreliable transport and communications.
- Skill constraints to absorptive capacity and technological learning.
- A complex and ambiguous tax regime.
- Lack of clear and enforceable property rights.
- Unclear contractual and other commercial relations.
- Corruption.
- Uncertain application of official policies on investment.
- Potential political instability between the mainland and Zanzibar.
- Weak political parties in opposition.
- Religious tensions.

Tanzania's public spending on investment in human capital formation is among the lowest in the world. In 1993 (where comparative data are available), public expenditure on education as a percentage of GDP was only 2.8 percent for Tanzania, compared with 5.3 percent for Kenya and 6.8 percent for Côte d'Ivoire. Analogously, in 1996 Tanzania's gross enrollment ratio for secondary schools was 5 percent compared with 12 percent for Uganda, 24 percent for Kenya, and an average of 27 percent for Sub-Saharan Africa, and 69 percent for East Asia. One key lesson that can be drawn from the East Asian growth miracle is that investment in human capital is key in driving the growth process insofar as it affects the development of entrepreneurial, management, and organizational skills as well as innovation and adaptation of new technology and modern practices. Thus, Tanzania's ability to join the group of strongly performing economies and to sustain growth that is high enough to decrease poverty will depend on the country's ability to expand educational opportunities and achievement. Privately provided and financed education will have a major role to play in meeting the demands of the economy for a cadre of well-trained engineers, applied scientists, and doctors as well as at managers in the private and public sectors.

FDI in Tanzania is low but on the rise. Improvements in the investment climate are clearly reflected in a significant rise of Tanzania in various country ratings and a matching increase in FDI. The country has been able to participate to a larger extent in the tremendous surge in FDI globally in recent years than most countries in Sub-Saharan Africa. Net FDI as a percentage of GDP for Tanzania increased from 0.3 percent in 1992 to 2.1 percent in 1998, compared with an average increase of 0.1 percent and 1.1 percent, respectively, for Sub-Saharan Africa. Considering that Tanzania is likely to face high competition for FDI from the emerging economies of Eastern Europe, it must work to create an environment that is conducive to attracting foreign capital and ODA. Again, this requires sustaining the economic and institutional reforms that are already under way.

The propensity to save remains low. In spite of the recent upward trend, occasioned by the recovery of private savings and achievement of a recurrent budget surplus since 1996, domestic savings are low both in absolute terms (6 percent of GDP) and relative to investment requirements. Such savings are also low when compared with strongly performing economies in Sub-Saharan Africa. Tanzania has recorded little progress in deposit mobilization following financial sector liberalization. Consequently, foreign savings rather than domestic savings have been the principal source of investment finance, thereby perpetuating dependency on foreign financing. Savings mobilization is severely constrained by the low level of development of the financial market, which is still characterized by limited competition, a large wedge between lending and deposit rates, market fragmentation, and a narrow range of available savings instruments.

Structural transformation is feasible in Tanzania. The main conclusion of this analysis is that Tanzania's industrialization strategy did not fail purely because of an inherent lack of international competitiveness, but rather because of policy mistakes and failure to react to market signals. Thus, the country has a huge potential for economic growth based on the private sector and market mechanisms, if the lessons from the failure of industrialization efforts in the 1970s are taken into account.

Growth in Tanzania's main trading partners exerts a significant influence on economic growth in the country (see figure 3.3). The two periods of economic slowdown in the late 1980s and early 1990s coincided with recessionary tendencies in Tanzania's trading partners in the Organization for Economic Co-operation and Development. To enable Tanzania to benefit from positive growth impulses from abroad and to minimize the negative impact from an economic slowdown abroad, the incentive regime and economic policies need to provide the economy with the flexibility to adjust to foreign growth impulses. However, while foreign factors contribute significantly to economic fluctuations in Tanzania in the medium term, average long-term economic growth in Tanzania is determined by domestic factors such as investment in human and physical capital, factor productivity, and economic policies.

Figure 3.3. *Economic Growth Patterns in Tanzania and Its Trading Partners, 5-Year Average Growth Rates, 1960–98*
(percent)

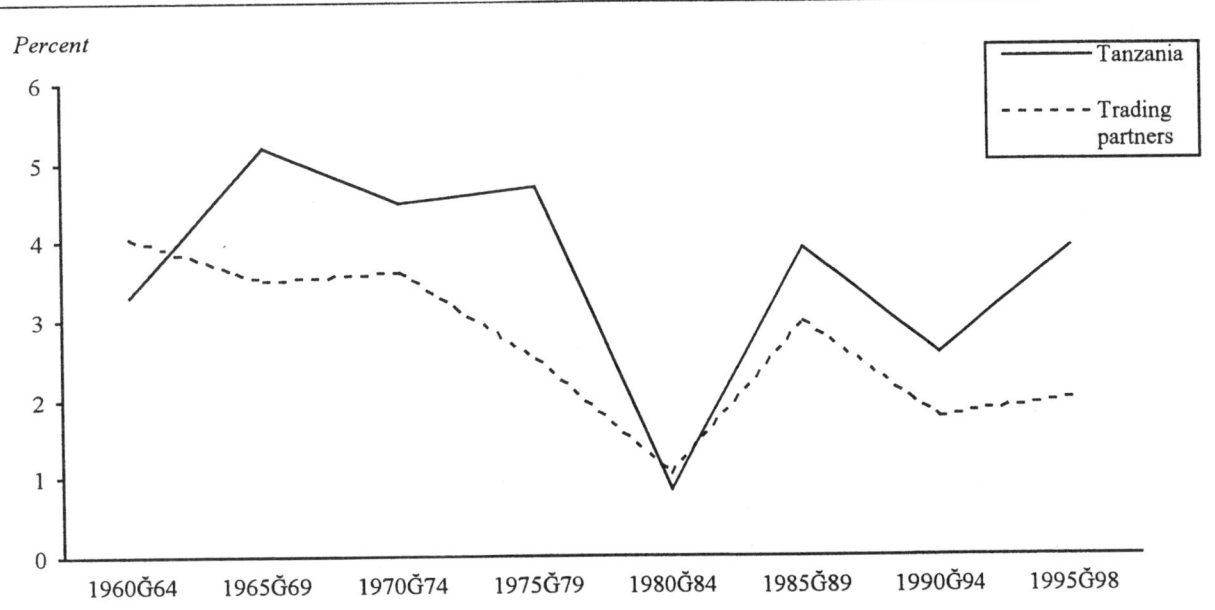

Growth spillovers within East Africa are smaller than the growth impulses originating from outside the region. However, there is clear evidence that such regional growth spillovers exist, with increased growth in neighboring countries exerting a positive impact on growth in Tanzania. Regional cooperation is thus important for economic growth in Tanzania. Measures to facilitate trade within the region, to improve regional infrastructure, and to create an investor-friendly environment in East Africa can be expected to provide significant benefits, including enhanced growth, for Tanzania and other countries of the subregion.

The governance approach followed by Tanzania before it adopted an open political regime in 1995 was not progrowth. Starting with a young political system at independence with weak institutional constraints on predatory behavior and pervasive rent-seeking, for three and a half decades Tanzania operated along neopatrimonial and autocratic lines. The initial preoccupation with building nationhood through the Africanization campaign, the protective stances on local economic activities, and the distribution of rents to maintain a delicate balance across interest groups preoccupied its policy and resource allocation, thereby limiting the adoption of pro-growth policies. There were also stringent limitations to mass political participation. In addition, the neopatrimonial regime had less control on the bureaucracy, which exerted excessive discretion. This led to an overextension of patron–client networks with large claims on dwindling public resources and control over other rent-earning avenues. The state had an overwhelming role in resource allocation and control over actions of economic agents. All this was done at the expense of a focus on growth.

4. COMBATING POVERTY, IGNORANCE, AND DISEASE

Four decades after independence, between 15 million and 18 million Tanzanians still live below the poverty line of US$0.65 a day. Of these, nearly 12.5 million live in abject poverty, spending less than US$0.50 on consumption a day. Poverty in Tanzania remains predominantly a rural phenomenon, although more recently the number of urban poor has been growing. These urban poor have mainly been the unemployed and those engaged in the informal sector. A combination of a rapid rate of migration into towns with a stagnant urban economy and rapid expansion of the labor force has led to rising unemployment, currently estimated at 30 percent of the labor force. The rural poor depend predominantly on agriculture to make a living; live in remote areas and in inhospitable agroclimatic zones; and typically are poor in productive assets, both physical and human. In contrast, the urban poor live in squalid conditions.

Children and the old also are afflicted with poverty, as reflected in the high dependence ratios. Nationally, on average, slightly more than 45 percent of the population is below the age of 15. The aging—those 65 or older—make up slightly more than 3 percent. Child dependency is greater than old-age dependency. The overall dependency ratio is high: 1.1. The rural survey by Research on Poverty Alleviation (1998) shows that poverty incidence is between 51 and 52 percent among the dependent age groups (those younger than 15 or those 65 years or older). It is also widely observed that poorer households tend to be larger than richer households.

The concern about poverty is not merely a welfare issue. It is also one of limiting the productive capacity of the economy. The poor are typically less educated, less healthy, and have larger families than those who are better off financially. Adjusted data from the household budget survey of fiscal 1992 indicate several things about the poor. First, the incidence of poverty (basic needs) is highest among households with their own farms (57 percent), followed by those economically inactive (53 percent), the self-employed (27 percent), and the employed (17 percent). Second, the incidence of poverty is highest for households with no formal education (61 percent) and falls with a higher level of educational attainment (for example, poverty incidence is only 8 percent among those with education level 5 or higher). Third, poverty incidence rises with the dependency ratio, from 32 percent for a 0–0.25 dependency ratio to 56 percent for a 0.75–1.0 dependency ratio. Fourth, incidence of poverty rises with the size of the household. Poverty exists in only 6 percent of households with 1 member, but in 67 percent of households with 10 or more members. Fifth, poverty falls with a larger proportion of household members' being employed. The incidence of poverty is high (58 percent) for households with no members employed, but low (18 percent) for households with four or more members employed. These dimensions of poverty curtail the capacity of the poor to engage in income generation, throwing them into a vicious circle of poverty. Reducing poverty and improving social conditions therefore ought to be viewed as part of a growth and development strategy.

For the past four decades, poverty reduction has been on Tanzania's policy agenda, with significant variation in form and content. However, economic growth was not emphasized as a means for raising private incomes and public revenues needed for sustainable financing of the poverty reduction programs. At independence, three arch enemies of economic growth were declared to be poverty, ignorance, and disease. The development strategy adopted then focused on their elimination. Poverty as a central development concern received a sharper focus after the adoption of a socialist strategy in 1967 and dominated the central government investment programs during the 1970s, with emphasis on expanding facilities for delivery of basic social services: education, health, and water. The basic needs approach to development programming, which was then high on the global development agenda, underpinned this strategy. Indeed, by the early 1980s, rather ambitious targets were adopted to achieve primary education, health, and water for all. These efforts drew significant support from donor financing. The strategic emphasis during the first two decades of independence was thus placed on raising public consumption of basic services, financed mainly through income redistribution and aid; and on raising private consumption of basic goods through subsidies, price controls, or both. Less emphasis was placed on economic growth as a means for raising private incomes and public revenues needed for sustainable financing of the poverty reduction programs.

Although overall human development is significantly higher currently than it was at independence, the rapid rate of improvement achieved until the early 1980s has slowed down. Further retrogression is expected in primary school enrollment, and possibly in life expectancy, as the spread of the AIDS pandemic threatens to erode past achievements in human development. Important, rapid improvements in human development were achieved during the first two decades. Primary-school enrollment rose rapidly from 25 percent of school-aged children at independence to 93 percent in 1980. Adult illiteracy fell sharply from 80 percent at independence to 5 percent in 1985. Access to primary health facilities and medical personnel improved rapidly with the growth of dispensaries and health centers, from a total of 1,210 in 1961 to 2,839 in 1980. Population coverage by medical personnel rose sharply from 1 physician for every 21,000 people in 1960 to 1 physician for every 15,000 people in 1997. The number of nurses increased from 1 for every 10,000 people in 1960 to 1 for every 5,000 in 1997. The access to piped water also improved, from about 750,000 Tanzanians in 1961 to at least 10 million Tanzanians in 1980. For a country whose per capita income rate increased only by 30 percent between 1961 and 1985, these achievements were indeed spectacular.

The rapid deterioration of the facilities for delivery of social services since the early 1980s, along with the inability to keep pace with the needs of the rapidly expanding population, is mainly due to a mismatch between the pace of these achievements and deceleration of growth. The previous fast improvement in human development could not be sustained, because the growth necessary for underpinning such progress was lacking. To a large extent, investment finance for the expansion of facilities depended on aid resources, and was thus less constrained. Maintenance and operations, in contrast, is mainly the responsibility of the government. With a declining tax base due to poor growth and a mushrooming underground economy (outside the tax net), the resource base for financing maintenance and operations was severely constrained. Austerity programs associated with macroeconomic stabilization and higher debt servicing obligations during the subsequent period exacerbated this financing pressure.

The government has resumed its focus on poverty reduction after a decade of preoccupation with reestablishing macroeconomic stability and structural reforms aimed at creating an enabling environment for growth. Tanzania faces massive challenges to sustain gains made in improving the human development status. This renewal is part of a global effort for a sustainable exit from the poverty trap. The global effort finds expression in the 1995 World Summit on Social Development, the 1997 UNDP paper on poverty eradication, the 1997 United Kingdom white paper on international development, the Development Assistance Committee (of the Organisation for Economic Co-operation and Development) targets for the 21st century, the Second Tokyo International Conference on African Development 1998, and the enhanced HIPC Initiative in 1999. International development targets flowing from these summits focus on poverty reduction and are part of the renewed interest in addressing the poverty problem in a sustainable manner. They combine sustaining growth and redressing extreme inequalities, combine public and private sector initiatives, and place greater emphasis on effective service delivery as well as accountability.

Tanzania is party to these international initiatives and has committed itself to achieving the international targets. The government has undertaken to prepare a poverty reduction strategy, a crucial part of the HIPC development program. Preparations for an effective poverty monitoring system are also under way. Through the Public Service Reform Program, the government has emphasized improved public service delivery. This is to be done through performance improvement and a results orientation, rationalization of public service functions, and an enhanced meritocratic incentive system. The government adopted the approach of using an MTEF for allocating resources that have strategic priority. This approach focuses on poverty reduction in budgets that also ensure sustainable investment. This budget management system will be embedded in an overall development strategy (the TAS) that also coordinates external assistance. Prospectively, Tanzania will benefit from the poverty-focused, enhanced HIPC Initiative. Finally, the recent adoption of decentralized public service delivery is aimed at raising effectiveness, taking public choices closer to the stakeholders, and promoting improved accountability.

If the renewed effort toward poverty reduction is to succeed, the strategic approaches have to incorporate lessons from past failure to sustain improvements in human development. Two questions arise from that experience, even as growth resumes and aid flows improve. Had Tanzania embarked on an unsustainable rate of improvement in the quality of life relative to its income level? Is the current retrogression in some key indicators of human development a process of returning these achievements to a level commensurate with the country's income? The answers to these two questions will temper the ambition of regaining past achievements in a hurry, even in the context of the recent renewed focus on poverty reduction. Analysis that estimates the expected status of human development indicators for Tanzania's income level on the basis of international experience concludes that Tanzania's achievements exceeds expectations.

There is now significant evidence that, in general, growth is essential for reducing poverty on a sustained basis. However, a growing economy offers opportunities for the poor to earn a decent income, if growth is also widely spread and occurs in those sectors on which the poor depend the most. As Eele and others (1999) show, a 1 percent increase in GDP reduces the proportion of those below the poverty line by 0.8 percent, whereas a reduction of the Gini coefficient (through redistribution of income) by 1 percent reduces poverty by only 0.15 percent. Although the impact of growth on poverty reduction is more powerful than redistributional interventions in Tanzania, growth needs to be complemented by actions that redress gross inequalities in earning capacities and opportunities across geographical locations, socioeconomic groupings, and gender. Such actions should take into account who the poor are and the reasons for their being trapped in poverty. The design of effective safety nets for the most vulnerable depends also on such information. Furthermore, the analysis in this chapter points to the need to pay attention to the high population dependency ratio, which places an unsustainable burden on the productive labor force to fend for minors and the elderly. An accelerated demographic transition enables higher savings, and therefore investment and growth.

Problems of Analyzing Poverty in Tanzania

A significant problem with the analytical work on poverty in Tanzania is a lack of a consistent and comparable definition of the status of poverty that can be used to assess changes over time. This lack is mainly due to differences in definitions of consumption baskets, population coverage, and sample sizes, as well as consistent valuation of expenditures. Recent techniques have been applied in Tanzania to quantify poverty so as to inform policymakers on the extent of the problem, its spatial dimensions, and differential incidence across social groups (for example, gender) and other characteristics of poverty. Quantification exercises, especially those involving computation of the national poverty line and related indexes of poverty using survey data, have not been without controversy. Most survey studies are at pains to portray their results as being as nationally representative as possible. Nevertheless, conclusions about the pervasiveness and depth of poverty are not controversial, and the determinants of poverty or factors are highly correlated (associated) with poverty where the different poverty lines have been used and cross-matched with the factors suspected to be related to poverty.

Apart from the measures based on the poverty line, the other approach to quantitative analysis of poverty in Tanzania that goes beyond the approach of private consumption expenditure uses the human development index (HDI) as applied by, for example, the UNDP. The index combines measures of literacy, life expectancy, and income into a single aggregate index. Income poverty and HDI approaches are complemented by analyses of other subjective, not strictly economic, aspects, such as leisure, personal security and esteem, social rights, services from common property, and the like. Studies that use more anthropological and sociological methods collectively called "participatory poverty appraisal" try to capture these dimensions of livelihood. The debate is not carried too far regarding which of the approaches—income or expenditure on poverty, HDI, or participatory appraisal—is more adequate than the other but, because of the underlying philosophical differences, the three approaches can sometimes generate conflicting results.

Human Development

4.13   Despite overall improvement in the HDI between 1991 and 1999, relative to global achievements, Tanzania's rank has declined over the same period. The HDI combines life expectancy, the literacy rate, and income. HDI has been used to rank countries, with indexes scaled between 0 and 1, where a value of 1 indicates better performance in terms of life expectancy, income, and literacy. Table 4.1 shows the HDI indexes for Tanzania and the country's ranking on the world scale for 1991–99. The index rose by 58 percent (an average of 5 percent per year relative to 1991), but the country slid 29 places down the global scale. Other countries have been making faster gains recently relative to Tanzania.

Table 4.1. *Tanzania's Human Development Index, Per Capita Income, and Ranking, 1991–99*

Economic indicator	1991	1992	1993	1994	1995	1996	1997	1998	1999
HDI	0.266	0.268	0.270	0.306	0.364	0.364	0.357	0.358	0.421
Rank by HDI (out of 174 countries)	127[a]	126[a]	138[b]	148[b]	147	144	149	150	156
Per capita income (US$)	180.7	167.0	149.2	156.2	176.9	210.3	235.6	257.0	270.0

a. Out of 160 countries.
b. Out of 173 countries.
Sources: United Nations Development Programme, *Human Development Reports* (various); Bank of Tanzania *Economic Bulletin* (various).

Tanzania's index is just below the Sub-Saharan Africa average of 0.463. The index for all developing countries is 0.637. In 1999, Tanzania ranked 156th out of 174 countries, down from 126th in 1990. It is noteworthy, however, that relative to its rank of fifth poorest country globally for income per capita, Tanzania's rank in HDI is far above expectations (see figure 4.1). Empirical evidence shows that, on average, a country's HDI ranking corresponds to its ranking by income per capita, making income the most dominant component in the index. Tanzania's better ranking in HDI relative to its income may be attributed to its more egalitarian policies of the past and the high aid dependence in financing social sector investments. The latter reason, however, raises the question of sustainability of this achievement in the absence of robust growth.

Inequality

Two ways of looking at inequality in Tanzania are used here. The first is overall income inequality (as also manifested by differences in consumption expenditures). However, rather than inequality in income (expenditures), a second approach seeks to explain inequality in the observed distribution of factors that are strongly correlated to income. These have to do with, for example, opportunities for generating income and differences in access to education, physical assets, credit, and natural resources. Inequality is reckoned to have increased in Tanzania between 1969 and 1991 as the Gini coefficient rose from 0.39 in FY1969, to 0.44 in FY1977, and to 0.57 in FY1991. Overall, between 1991 and 1993, inequality declined by 5 percent in Tanzania, while rural inequality declined by about 6 percent. However, after 1993 inequality increased again. The surveys (for example, World Bank 1993) indicate that the average expenditure per capita and per adult for the better-off households is 6 to 7 times higher than those of the poor and 8 to 10 times those of the "very poor." The rural survey (Research on Poverty Alleviation 1998) indicates that the top 20 percent of the population surveyed accounts for 45 percent of the (mean) expenditures. The lowest quintile accounted for only 6 percent. Those in the highest quintile spend seven times more than those in the lowest quintile. The socioeconomic groups face different hurdles, and so the gaps are still a reality.

Figure 4.1. *Human Development Index: Comparison between Tanzania and Neighboring Countries, 1999*

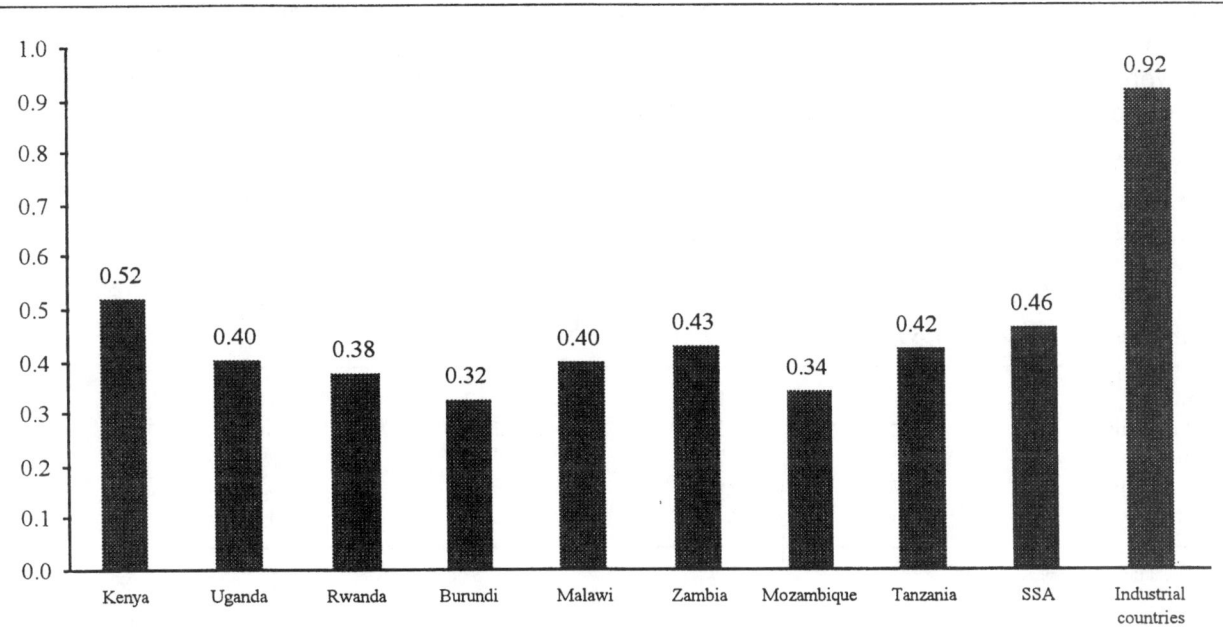

The most apparent sources of income inequalities over the 1990s have their roots in the differential access to productive assets, including education, and land and livestock ownership, which mostly reflect the intrarural inequalities, with a Gini coefficient as high as 0.8 (World Bank 1996; Research on Poverty Alleviation 1998; URT 1999a,b,c). Generally, the poor hold less land in terms of acreage, the quality of their land is poor, and they can ill-afford acquisition of farm implements, inputs, and credit. The poor are also less educated and their educational attainment has worsened over time. Although evidence from the 1991 household consumption survey suggests that 54.3 percent of the rural poor were literate (could read and write) compared with 61 percent for the rural population as a whole in 1991, between 1983 and 1991 illiteracy among the poor increased, while the proportion of illiterate women remained more or less the same, but still higher than any socioeconomic group. As evidenced by the Human Resources Development Survey (HRDS) for 1993/94, gross enrollment rates among poor children aged 7–9 also decreased, falling from 82 percent in 1983 to 80 percent in 1993.

Income (income poverty) also varies widely across the country. Data for 1997 indicate the per capita income of the better-off region to be 3.9 times higher than that of the poorest region. The four most deprived regions on the basis of this indicator were Kilimanjaro, Dodoma, Kigoma, and Kagera. It has been argued that the Kilimanjaro, and Kagera regions are better judged by their GNP rather than GDP because of significant transfers that they receive from urban residents. By the same measure, the least deprived regions were Dar es Salaam, Rukwa, Arusha, and Iringa.

On the basis of a composite deprivation index—which takes into account food security, income and production, education, health status, nutrition, water, and health services—the most deprived regions are Dodoma, Kagera, Lindi, Kigoma, and Coast. The least deprived regions are Dar es Salaam, Ruvuma, Kilimanjaro, Singida, and Tabora. As regards food security, estimates based on cereal equivalent levels indicate Tanga, Morogoro, Dodoma, Coast, and Lindi to be the most deprived regions. The most vulnerable districts include Tanga, Lushoto, Handeni, Ulanga, Dodoma Rural, Bagamoyo, Kilwa, Liwale, Makete, and Ngorongoro (URT 1999b).

Lack of access and inadequate resource endowments at the household level has not only led to income inequality, but also to localized food insecurity and hunger. HRDS data confirm increased an incidence of malnutrition among the poorest children between 1991 and 1996 (table 4.2). Rates of infant mortality are also higher for the poor, particularly in rural areas, than for the general population. Infant mortality seems to have worsened between 1991 and 1996 for the poorest quintile (table 4.3). Mortality rates for children under the age of three have improved, but remain high.

Table 4.2. *Percentage of Children Malnourished by Asset Index Quintile, 1991 and 1996*

	Height for age, stunting		Weight for age, wasting	
Asset index quintile	1991	1996	1991	1996
First quintile	43.14	46.02	8.12	8.18
Second quintile	43.52	43.98	6.73	9.82
Third quintile	42.97	41.79	5.27	9.02
Fourth quintile	40.12	39.00	6.22	8.89
Fifth quintile	26.06	28.42	6.83	6.24

Source: Sahn, Stifel, and Younger (1999).

Table 4.3. *Infant and Under-Age-Three Mortality by Asset Index Quintile, 1991 and 1996*

	Infant mortality		Under-age-three mortality	
Asset index quintile	1991	1996	1991	1996
First quintile	113.7	116.2	155.6	144.1
Second quintile	112.0	103.2	168.3	144.1
Third quintile	97.4	88.5	152.4	138.0
Fourth quintile	87.7	99.9	141.3	153.3
Fifth quintile	75.9	66.1	126.6	91.2

Source: Sahn, Stifel, and Younger (1999).

The other type of inequality that is not necessarily reflected in the Gini coefficient is that relating to gender imbalance. Recent analysis based on data from the household budget survey (FY92) indicates that the proportion of male-headed and female-headed households below the poverty line are 49 percent and 45 percent, respectively (NBS 2000). This conclusion contradicts earlier evidence based on data from the participatory poverty appraisal survey (see, for example, World Bank 1996), which had shown that households headed by women (especially in rural areas) were more likely to be poorer than male-headed households. This is basically because female-headed households tend to have fewer assets—land and livestock—and tend to have fewer years of schooling and higher dependency ratios. The National Bureau of Statistics results are interesting and do actually point to an important policy implication regarding the context of the position of a woman in a society. This relates to the fact that where formal gender-based discrimination does not exist, women tend to occupy a better position economically. However, since traditional and cultural barriers still assign the male dominance role in day-to-day decisions of the majority of Tanzanian families, the main concerns that have been echoed regarding the position of a woman in the society are still applicable.

Gender imbalance in disfavor of females in education has been particularly sharp for postprimary education. Up the schooling ladder, from primary school to the university level, the representation of female students as a percentage of total student population declines. Policy initiatives by both government and nongovernmental bodies targeting reduction of gender imbalances should seek to remove barriers to educational attainment and address the issue of property ownership and inheritance for women.

Gross Enrollment Compared with Educational Attainment

Generally, the educational attainment of children in Tanzania is poor and was deteriorating during the 1990s. The deterioration has occurred basically because of three significant problems with education in Tanzania (IDA and IMF 2000). First is the rapid deterioration in the enrollment rates during primary school: entry rates are relatively high (nearly 90 percent), but survival rates at the end of the cycle are low (54 percent). The problem is more acute for children from poorer and female-headed households. The second significant concern is Tanzania's low enrollment rate in secondary and tertiary education, compared with other countries with a similar level of income. A principal reason for this is affordability: the cost of secondary and tertiary education is high relative to income levels in Tanzania. The low student–teacher ratio, high overheads (for example, because of boarding and related subsidies, which are disproportionately enjoyed by the better off), and low use of facilities combine to raise unit costs. Third, although the overall budget provision for education in Tanzania (at about 2.5 percent of GNP) is comparable to that in other low-income countries, subsector allocations and cost-effectiveness in delivery remain significant obstacles to reaching the poor.

Although assessing achievement in education on the basis of gross enrollment has been one of the main problems, educational attainment has recently become an even bigger and more fundamental problem. It is also the case that the effect of education on growth is most commonly assessed in terms of attainment rather than enrollment. Filmer (1999), on the basis of data on educational attainment for children aged 15–19 in Tanzania and using 1996 as a sample year, observed that the pattern of educational attainment varies greatly across the population, with different groups displaying a variety of profiles in attainment (figure 4.2). Overall, about 90 percent of children aged 15–19 complete grade 1. The ratio of those who attain the next grade to those who do not changes over time as a result of dropout. The ratio for grade 4 is 75 percent, while only about 50 percent complete grade 7 (figure 4.2a).

There are also interesting differences in educational attainment patterns. These differences are based on the wealth status of various groups. For example, the attainment of children from the richest 20 percent is strikingly different from that of the poorest 40 percent. About 80 percent of the poor complete grade 1, whereas almost 100 percent of the rich do so (figure 4.2e). These differences increase over time, with only 40 percent of the poor (and almost an equal proportion of the middle class) completing grade 7, compared with 75 percent of the rich. This indicates that shortfalls in universal primary completion are, for the most part, due to children from the poorest households not completing target levels of schooling.

Educational attainment also differs by gender. The attainment ratio for grade 1 is about 95 percent for males and 85 for females. For grade 4, the ratio, although lower, is the same—at 80 percent for both genders (figure 4.2b). However, for subsequent grades, the attainment ratio falls further down, but remains higher for females (55 percent) compared with males (45 percent). This pattern does not seem to change, even when the attainments are compared on the basis of a combination of gender and wealth status (figure 4.2f). Girls seem to be performing better up to grade 7, for both rich and poor groups. However, their dropout ratio rises sharply after grade 7. Better performance for girls than boys up to grade 7 can be explained by the relatively poorer school attendance by boys, particularly in urban areas. Recent evidence, for example, shows that, on average, girls in the 7–15 age category residing in urban areas, are 8 percentage points more likely to attend primary school than boys, other factors being equal (Al-Samarrai, Donecker, and Reilly forthcoming). The strong urban effect may reflect two things: first, the opportunity cost of attending primary school, which is lower for girls in urban areas given that foregone hours of household activity, may be more highly valued in rural areas; and second, boys have better access to labor market opportunities than girls.

Figures 4.2. *Tanzania: Educational Attainment for the 15–19 Age Group, 1996*

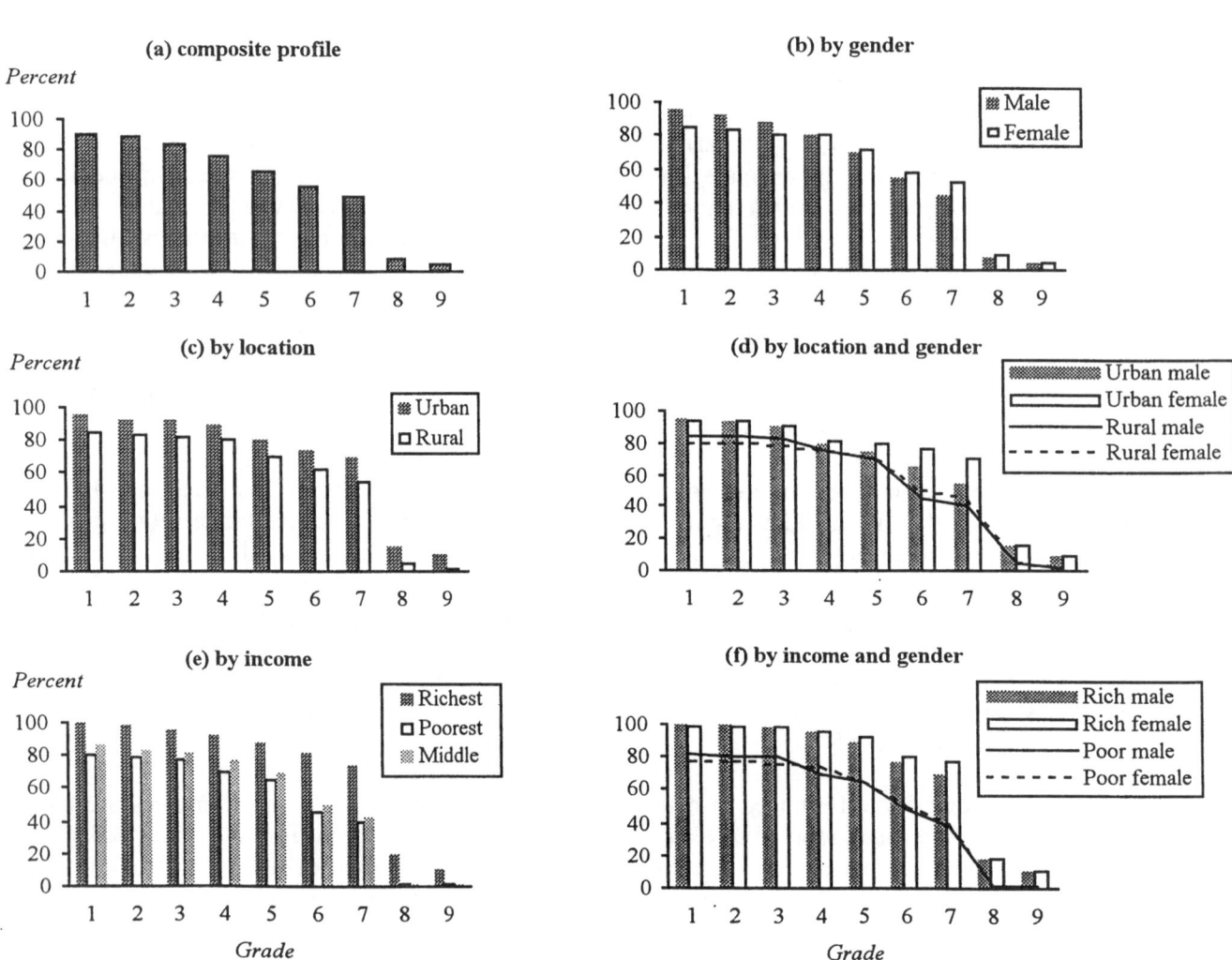

38

Educational attainment also differs enormously among various groups on the basis of their location. Educational attainment seem to be higher for urban children compared with rural children (Figure 4.2c). The attainments for urban and rural areas are, respectively, about 95 percent and 85 percent for grade 1, about 90 percent and 80 percent for grade 4, and about 70 percent and 55 percent for grade 7. Again, girls seem to be performing better than boys up to grade 7, for both urban and rural groups, although the dropout ratio for girls rises sharply after grade 7.

Filmer's (1999) analysis also compares primary-level educational attainments for groups aged 20–29 and 30–39 in 1996 (figure 4.3). The former group attended primary school between the mid-1970s and the early 1980s, while the latter group went to primary school between the mid-1960s and mid-1970s. Filmer then compares the educational attainment of the two groups with that of the 15–19 age group to gauge whether any significant change has occurred in educational attainment over the past 30–40 years. The following observations are clear. First, enrollment in grade 1 increased over time, from about 75 percent during the mid-1960s through the mid-1970s, to about 85 percent during the mid-1970s through the early 1980s, and about 90 percent in the mid-1980s through the late 1980s. Second, educational attainment to the grade 7 level has fluctuated over time, declining (from more dropouts) in recent years. It rose from about 60 percent in the mid-1960s through the mid-1970s to 70 percent during the mid-1970s through the early 1980s, but declined to about 50 percent in the mid-1980s through the late 1980s. Third, the difference in educational attainment based on gender has declined substantially over time (figures 4.2b, 4.3b, and 4.3d). The improvement is substantial, and as noted earlier, is marked by better performance by girls up to grade 7.

Figures 4.3. *Tanzania: Educational Attainment for the 20–29 and 30–39 Age Groups, 1996*

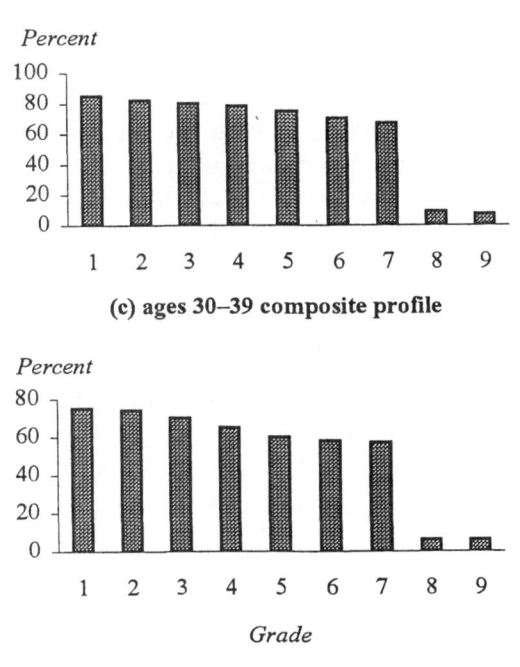

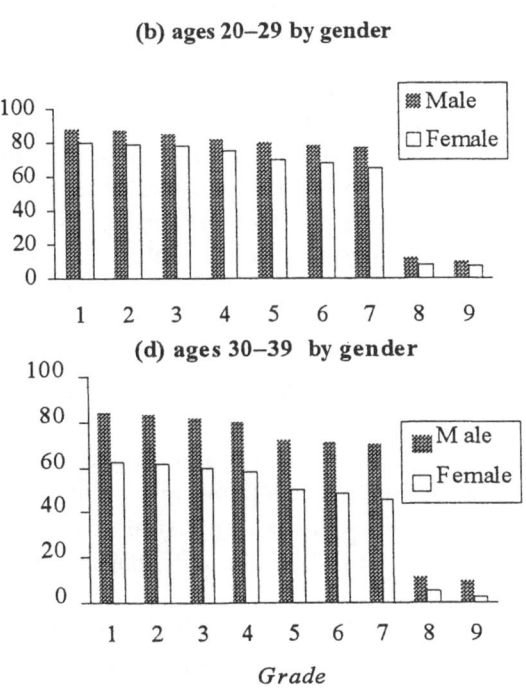

Grade

39

Imperatives for Strategic Action to Reduce Poverty

4.28   In light of the pervasiveness of poverty and its multidimensional character, the action program needs to be frontal in its approach, that is, it must emphasize improving income opportunities as the most sustainable way toward Tanzania's Vision 2025 targets. The starting point is to recognize that, given the breadth of poverty, action would need to focus on creating and expanding opportunities for the poor to earn a decent income and thus to enable their access to the essentials of life. This focus is based on the belief that reducing poverty on a sustained basis, when it is both broad and deep, pivots around enabling the poor to earn a decent income, rather than solely on public transfers, important as they may be in the interim period and for addressing the needs of vulnerable groups. This does not necessarily mean that programs targeted at the most vulnerable of the poor are not essential. It does mean accepting the fact that, with slightly more than half of the population being below the poverty line, a broad strategy needs to be adopted.

In the Tanzanian context, safety nets are organized around informal private networks. Safety nets that are publicly financed ought to focus on the old and orphans not supported under such networks as well as on consequences of disasters that typically affect whole geographic zones. Identification of zones most highly at risk climatically would be particularly useful in the latter case. Moreover, measures to improve income opportunities for the poor would need to be anchored in macroeconomic policies aimed at maintaining a low inflation rate and overall fiscal discipline; at improving the incentive framework for private investment, particularly in agriculture; and at providing supportive infrastructure to small enterprises in the informal sector in both rural and urban areas.

Capabilities for designing operational programs for poverty reduction and for monitoring implementation are key for successful interventions. One of the main impediments to the design and execution of poverty-reducing programs has been a lack of supportive analytical capacity and good data, at the country level, that are in an easy-to-use form. The presence of this competence and organized information on poverty profiles and the structure of poverty is necessary not only for careful selective targeting in line with resource constraints, but also for performance monitoring. The government prepared and approved a National Poverty Eradication Strategy (URT 1998a) after widespread consultations. The government has also developed a framework and indicators for monitoring poverty, but lacks data to make it operational. A lack of local technical support for the programs has meant that advice is sporadic, when it is available from outside; monitoring is not continuous; and design is largely based on guesswork. Investment in this competence locally is important for sustained action, particularly where the targeted programs that are more demanding are concerned.

Three broad areas of needed action in this respect are

- Strengthening local analytic capacity for research and policy analysis in support of formulation of appropriate interventions and policies for reducing poverty.
- Rationalizing state responsibilities for selecting and analyzing information on poverty.
- Transferring skills through appropriate technical assistance.

Local analytical skills are needed for analyzing poverty profiles and their changes over time for monitoring and targeting purposes; for explaining the main causes of poverty in the specific context so as to enable prioritization of action; and for assessing options for action in terms of potential effectiveness for given resource envelopes. Even where data pertaining to poverty exist, these have largely remained unused because the skills and knowledge needed to analyze them are lacking. It is highly unlikely that such capacity will reside in the institutions housing the main actors. A networking approach among research and other academic institutions (where most analysts reside), professionals in concerned public policy institutions, and activist groups will provide the necessary framework for dividing roles.

Competence in absorbing and applying knowledge to programs and interventions should be strengthened in the using institutions.

The second area where action is needed is rationalizing the operations of state institutions responsible for collecting information pertinent to analyzing and monitoring poverty. The bureau of statistics regularly collects and organizes information on the status of living conditions from household budget surveys, the population census, and other data sources. These contain valuable information for required analysis of poverty and its determinants. An important improvement would be to anticipate data needs for such analysis in the design of surveys, in close consultation with analysts and researchers. However, even more important would be the removal of impediments to the timely access of information collected, to be able to use this information for policy analytical purposes and to assess the design and impact of interventions. Most urgent is the need to undertake a new household budget survey to set up a base for the poverty reduction programs and for monitoring implementation. This is also necessary for the design and monitoring of a poverty-focused HIPC initiative.

The third area pertains to setting up mechanisms for the effective transfer of knowledge from experts availed through technical assistance to local experts. To this end, monitorable mechanisms of such transfer must be provided formally, through technical assistance packages, with assessment at the conclusion of support. Careful selection of understudies with the capability to absorb the knowledge is crucial for success, and so is the selection of experts involved in the technical assistance. To this end, the ability and willingness to teach others should be important criteria in selecting the experts. This mechanism for transfer of knowledge could be linked to the wider network of researchers and analysts so as to broaden benefits from it and raise the scope for retaining the skills availed.

Investment in a healthy and educated work force is not only important to overall growth of the economy, but also enhances the capacity of the poor to earn a decent income. Giving a greater priority in the allocation of public spending to social sectors and more efficient delivery of these services is crucial for enhancing the human capital of the poor and their welfare. Improvement in human capabilities is crucial for raising productivity, and hence incomes, of the poor. Better education, health, and nutrition are not simply definitions of welfare status, but also crucial human capital for sustaining this status through growth. They constitute important inputs into human assets for earning an income.

Until recently, public spending on education and health has been inadequate, as reflected by declining real expenditure per person, and now needs to be given the highest priority. The problem has been due both to the small size of the discretionary resource envelope after servicing debt obligations and to not giving the social sector the highest priority in expenditure allocations. Social sector objectives must be consistent with macroeconomic realities. However, the share of the budget destined for the social sectors, and the effort to integrate government and donor funds more fully into the poverty strategy, must be increased. Making room for a larger share of public spending to these sectors will require debt relief as well as continued scaling down of government involvement in commercial and noncore activities. This can be achieved through continued implementation of the privatization program, the public service rationalization program, and enhanced HIPC Initiative debt relief. Furthermore, strengthening budget management would ensure that funds earmarked for poverty programs actually are spent on them. Perhaps what is even more crucial now is pursuing cost-effectiveness in achieving well-defined goals. Expenditure reviews that incorporate assessment of the cost-effectiveness and impact of previous budgets should form an important basis for approving new budgets in support of poverty reduction.

The involvement of the state in poverty-reducing programs is not limited to public expenditure programs or provision of public services. To a large extent, the effectiveness of the state's contribution hinges on creating an enabling environment for other actors and promoting a sense of urgency in dealing with the problem of poverty. Its own commitment to raising the welfare of the poor is an important signal to the rest of the society and should be reflected partly by the extent of priority it gives welfare of the poor in its budget and the efficiency with which it applies resources to eradicate poverty. It should also be reflected by the vigor with which it pursues promotion of market efficiency in support of poverty-reducing private expenditures and regulates providers against exploiting information failures to the detriment of the welfare status of the country.

Public action, however, is not confined to provision of these services. It includes encouraging other providers and having an effective regulatory framework against malpractice and to counter information failures. Public provision of education has faced problems related to underfunding of essential services and to cost-effectiveness. The earlier problem has come about because of budgetary constraints and allocations of limited budgetary resources that did not give priority to these sectors. The latter problem of low cost-effectiveness results from lack of prioritization in favor of services with high social returns and from failure to stem wastage of public resources, which raises the cost of services. A striking example here is overprescription of drugs ("polypharmacy") in Africa, where prescriptions required to achieve the same therapeutic effect have been assessed to be only 12 percent of actual use (Appleton and Mackinon 1996).

The main adjustments to current public policy practice include:

- Restructuring budgets in favor of primary and secondary education.
- Improving the flow of health information that is considered most effective for improving public health.
- Raising the quality of education by providing more inputs in the form of textbooks and other learning devices.
- Soliciting additional resources through user charges, provided they do not crowd out allocations from budgets and special provisions are made for the most vulnerable groups: orphans and the very poor.

Moreover, the recent trend toward decentralization of management of these services augurs well not only for enhanced accountability, and hence cost-effectiveness, but also for encouraging local initiatives. Decentralization will also assist in reducing the bias toward urban centers and enhance provision of these services to the rural areas, where the majority of the poor reside. Focusing public provision on rural areas complements the existing concentration of private services in urban centers.

The contribution of local communities as a framework for providing inexpensive education and, to a limited extent, primary health services, has grown in many countries and ought to be emulated in Tanzania. Harambee schools in Kenya provide a good example of mobilizing resources for education at the community level. Harambee (community fund raising) has also been used for collective financing of costs for tertiary education and expensive medical treatment when deemed necessary. Other forms of community support are organized under parental associations and women's organizations. Tanzania had aimed at promoting such arrangements of community involvement and ought now to raise their profile politically and in reality. These are worthwhile self-help traditions that ought to be promoted, and they provide a useful framework for assistance by governments and NGOs.

Public health education has proved effective for achieving impressive results in reducing mortality in countries such as China and Vietnam, where income levels remain low and comparable to those in many African countries. This information function remains quite weak in the prioritization of government spending in Tanzania. In light of tight budget constraints, giving higher priority to public health education will enhance the effectiveness of public resources in raising the health status of the majority of citizens. Successes of public awareness campaigns against the spread of communicable diseases, such as

HIV/AIDS, have been reported in countries where they have been vigorously promoted. Health codes enforced by local governments and rapid expansion of primary health care had played a pivotal role in the preindependence periods, and in the first decade after independence, in achieving a phenomenal reduction in mortality. The reappearance of some of the communicable diseases, long thought to have been eliminated, is partly due to relaxation of these efforts during the 1980s. Therefore, the government and nongovernmental organizations must reinvigorate health education and promote hygiene to avoid reversals of achievements from past efforts in this area and to consolidate gains made to date. Evidence based on regression analysis done on data from the Vice President's Office (URT 1999b) poverty profile point to the importance of immunizing infants and children under 5 years and improving the literacy levels of mothers if low birth weights and high mortality rates are to be reduced and life expectancy after birth increased. This underscores the importance of public health education on disease prevention and for improvements of nutritional status.

Poverty reduction is likely to be achieved faster if the poor are empowered, that is, given a voice in designing, implementing, and monitoring poverty alleviation measures. Good governance and accountability are also important in ensuring that earmarked funds reach the poor. Measures for improving governance include:

- Tracking public expenditure at all levels of government.
- Setting and monitoring priority indicators.
- Strengthening the regulatory framework in key markets to improve transparency and competition.
- Implementing programs for promoting the welfare of women and other groups that, for various reasons (for example, racial, or ethnic), do not fully participate in society (URT 1999a,b).

An important point to bear in mind in designing poverty reduction strategies is that the majority of the poor reside in rural areas and are primarily engaged in agriculture. In the case of the urban poor, the majority are engaged in the informal economy. The growth strategies to be adopted necessarily then have to place a high priority on addressing the geographic concentration of poverty and to uplifting productivity in these two critical sectors. The related investment in infrastructure to support production and market integration needs to be consistent with these locational and sectoral priorities.

The renewal of growth has to start at the countryside for it to begin to effectively make a dent in poverty. Previous attempts at agricultural transformation were frustrated by problems of poor design and implementation. State involvement substituted for grassroots initiatives, committed resources were inadequate, and policies heavily taxed agriculture in favor of failed industrialization in the form of import substitution (Ndulu and Van de Walle 1996). The past decade has seen a significant shift away from these problems, as market orientation took root. Some encouraging results in the upturn of the growth of the sector and productivity growth have been achieved (Delgado 1996; IFPRI and World Bank 2000). The focus now should be on pursuit of investment in new sources of productivity growth. This entails reducing transaction costs related to transport costs, facilitating the adoption of technological innovations to enhance supply responsiveness, and creating schemes aimed at reducing risks to enable specialization according to ecological comparative advantages. The next chapter of this memorandum gives more details on the imperatives for renewing agricultural growth in Tanzania.

The informal sector in Tanzania is probably the most dynamic and most important source of livelihood for the urban-dwelling poor. Tanzania ought to harness the dynamism and enthusiasm of this sector by removing impediments to its growth and by providing a framework for availing credit and supportive infrastructure to small enterprises and trading activities. The urban informal sector has been most noteworthy in grassroots efforts to cushion against declines in real incomes, even for those employed in the formal sector at the lower end of the pay scale. It is considered to be the most dynamic in terms of employment generation and productivity growth (World Bank 1998; Lall and Stewart 1996) and has thrived in spite of government restrictions. This sector's contributions to the public coffers can be elicited through less hostile means than curtailment of its activities. Indirect taxes have captured this source of income. Nongovernmental organizations have played an important role in the organizational improvements and business orientation of this sector, and more needs to be done by these entities in sharpening skills and enhancing the capacity of the sector to thrive.

Speeding up the demographic transition is necessary to reduce pressures on domestic resources that constrain them from being used to support poverty reduction programs. The pressure of rapid expansion of demands on the limited means of the economy, occasioned by the high population growth in the country and its high dependency structure, is a significant drawback to growth and poverty reduction. While in a few countries, demographic transition to lower population growth and a more mature age structure has begun, Tanzania, like the majority of African countries, has not embarked on a demographic transition. The problem of rapid population growth in Tanzania remains intact. Population policies and programs for encouraging people to have fewer children sprang up several years ago, but continue to be constrained by limited resources. Greater growth of the economy and of education are important elements in the effort to stem rapid growth of the population. However, the large contribution of population growth inertia to this problem, in spite of the actions described above, means that for the foreseeable future the country will have to contend with this problem from the side of higher economic growth and productivity to meet growing needs.

Combating HIV and AIDS

The HIV/AIDS epidemic is spreading rapidly in Tanzania. HIV infection already ranks as the top health problem among Tanzania's urban populations. As of December 1997, Tanzania was estimated to have 1.5 million productive adults infected with the deadly virus, with infection spreading at a high rate. The infection rate in urban centers is estimated to exceed 24 percent, and up to 10 percent in rural areas. The impact of the epidemic is devastating, given that it strikes adults in their prime years, including the elite and professionals. This implies that it kills workers of much greater than average productivity. Furthermore, it is estimated that by 2015 more people in rural areas than in urban areas will be infected with HIV, with a serious effect of reducing the agricultural labor force, and therefore production. Worse, more women are infected with HIV than men, the ratio being 1.5 to 1. This is important considering that women spend more time in production and reproduction activities than men. Thus, HIV/AIDS is not just a health problem, but a grave development problem. Virtually all sectors are experiencing a loss of experienced, trained professionals. Given the mortality rate increases, life expectancy is estimated to decline by almost a decade, and the population structure will shift toward the younger age. The country has also witnessed a large increase of AIDS orphans in the last few years. The estimated number of orphans since the beginning of the epidemic is 730,000.

Contraction of HIV is usually a consequence of sexual behavior. Therefore, it can be prevented through changes in sexual behavior and treatment of sexually transmitted diseases. Some effective interventions are effectively diagnosing and treating sexually transmitted diseases; promoting a reduction in the number of sexual partners; promoting condom use; providing information, education, and communication about the epidemic and its prevention; counseling and testing; using mass media to effectively distribute HIV/AIDS awareness messages; and promoting abstinence. Key factors that cause susceptibility and vulnerability to the spread of the epidemic also need to be determined so they can be addressed. Variables that have been identified as the key factors of vulnerability to HIV transmission are poverty, gender inequality, migration, and poor health.

HIV/AIDS has become a fast-spreading epidemic in Tanzania primarily because of poverty and gender inequality. Poverty makes HIV/AIDS education difficult because of high levels of illiteracy and little access to mass media, health, and educational services. Poverty directly exacerbates HIV transmission through prostitution and inferior health care. Poverty indirectly exacerbates HIV transmission by increasing migrant labor, family dissolution, and homelessness, all of which lead to a greater risk of someone's having multiple partners. Poor people are also less likely to take seriously an infection that takes years to kill its victims, as poor people are too focused on trying to survive on a day-to-day basis. The incubation period of the disease is shortened because of poor standards of nutrition, repeated infections, and limited access to medical care. A loss of an adult in a poor household drives the family into greater poverty. Poverty affects women most, thus their economic dependence on a man in a marriage or in sexual relations that are commercial and less formal is increased.

Women are particularly vulnerable to HIV because of biological and socioeconomic factors. Biologically, a woman can more easily get infected from each sexual encounter than a man can. Having gender-biased social roles also increases the vulnerability of women to HIV infection. Gender inequality in culture, wealth, power, and politics tends to keep women oppressed. Women are not able to force their partners to wear condoms, nor are they able to refuse to have conjugal relations with them. Reducing women's and men's risk of infection demands gender-based responses that focus on how the different social expectations, roles, status, and economic power of men and women affect, and are affected by, the epidemic.

Countries severely affected by HIV/AIDS will experience a large impact on their health sectors. Total national expenditure on health care will rise. Each adult HIV/AIDS case treated in the health care system absorbs about US$290 (about T Sh 232,000) in nursing and drug costs, and the cost for pediatric AIDS is about US$195 (about T Sh 156,000), according to the World Bank (1992). Lower-income households will be less able to cope with medical expenses and loss of income, which will lead to increased poverty and inequality. In economies in which the public sector bears a large proportion of medical costs, the government must make difficult decisions about how to finance medical expenditure as HIV/AIDS-related spending rises. Three types of care are available for AIDS patients: relief of symptoms, prevention of opportunistic illnesses, and antiretroviral treatments. Each of these different types of care bear a different cost, with antiretroviral treatments being prohibitively expensive. Evidence shows home-based care to be more cost-effective than hospital care in Tanzania (URT 1999c). The epidemic also has indirect costs:

- Costs of funerals and mourning.
- Lower nutritional status and poor health of children.
- Reduced schooling of children as income declines and demand for child labor increases.
- Reallocation of labor across household members to treat the terminally ill and to compensate for their lost labor.
- Sale of land or other assets.
- Dissolution or migration of the household.
- Burdens placed on relatives to help finance medical and funeral costs.

HIV/AIDS was the leading cause of death among adults aged 15–59 in Dar es Salaam, Hai, and Morogoro Rural in 1992–95 (Ministry of Health 1997). Currently AIDS, combined with tuberculosis, is the leading cause of death in all areas covered by the project, causing 50 percent of the deaths of both men and women for the 35–59 age group in Ilala and Temeke (Ministry of Health 1999). Ill health and death due to AIDS were reported to have reduced the agricultural labor force, productivity, and disposable incomes in many families and rural communities. A trend of declining GDP has been observed in the Kagera and Tanga regions, associating reduced agricultural production to the increase in the number of AIDS cases (Muhimbili Medical Center and National AIDS Control Program 1999).

The impact of the HIV/AIDS epidemic is devastating and poses a serious threat to productivity and growth in the future. It kills adults in the prime of their working and parenting lives, thereby reducing the labor force, impoverishing families, orphaning children, and destroying communities. The impact of the epidemic is through its effect on two key inputs—labor and capital—and the size and quality of the labor force and through changes in productivity. The effects of HIV/AIDS can be grouped into those associated with rising morbidity rates and those associated with rising mortality rates. With morbidity, the effect on labor productivity is negative: loss of labor from the sick and their caretakers. Health care expenditures increase, causing a negative savings effect and a decline in human capital investments. The population growth rate has declined because of the epidemic. While decreasing, the birth rate may ease pressure on economic resources; however, the death of experienced workers, as is the case in the HIV/AIDS epidemic, changes the composition of the labor force to younger, less experienced workers. This causes a decline in human capital stock, and thus in national output.

Without decisive policy action, HIV/AIDS may reduce Tanzania's GDP in 2010 by an estimated 15–25 percent in relation to a no-HIV/AIDS scenario, according to Cuddington (1993). The presence of AIDS is estimated to reduce the average real GDP growth rate in 1985–2010 from 3.9 percent to a range of 2.8–3.3 percent. Per capita income levels are expected to fall by between 0 and 10 percent. Per capita GDP is expected to be moderately affected because of the decrease in population growth rate. Bloom and Sachs (1998) show that the factors contributing to Africa's poor economic performances—that is, low life expectancies and extremely youth-heavy age distributions—are exacerbated by the HIV/AIDS epidemic.

HIV/AIDS control activities need to become an integral part of development policy and practice. The adverse impact of the disease on development calls for widening the response outside the health sector and supplementing the health intervention with interventions that address the socioeconomic determinants and consequences of HIV/AIDS. Therefore, HIV/AIDS needs to be featured in the context of other cross-sectoral topics, such as poverty alleviation, gender, youth, and population. With the negative consequences of AIDS on the labor force, policy initiatives to restore productivity and maintain the stock of human capital will be critical for achieving economic growth.

The National AIDS Control Program is in its Third Medium-Term Plan (1998–2002). The objectives of this third plan is to prevent transmission of HIV/AIDS and other sexually transmitted diseases; to protect and support vulnerable groups; to mitigate the socioeconomic impacts of HIV/AIDS; and to strengthen the capacity of institutions, communities, and individuals to arrest the spread of the epidemic and mitigate its impact. The program's strategy focuses on 11 priority areas for providing a framework for an expanded, multisectoral response to the HIV/AIDS epidemic in Tanzania:

- Reduce the number of cases of sexually transmitted diseases.
- Reduce unsafe sexual behavior among highly mobile population groups.
- Reduce the transmission of HIV and other sexually transmitted diseases among commercial sex workers.
- Reduce unsafe sexual behavior among the armed and security forces.
- Reduce the vulnerability of youth to HIV/AIDS and other sexually transmitted diseases
- Maintain safe blood transfusion services.
- Assist women commercial sex workers in poverty to develop alternative means of earning an income.
- Improve the well-being of people living with HIV/AIDS.
- Reduce unprotected sex among men with multiple partners.
- Improve educational opportunities, especially for girls.
- Reduce the vulnerability of women in an adverse cultural environment.

Use of the participatory rural appraisal technique is important in enabling communities to express their needs and concerns about the HIV/AIDS epidemic. A community will embrace what it considers important, so analysts should be informed about what the community perceives as vital and incorporate this into the strategies laid out above. Also, with the participatory rural appraisal technique, the communities can be informed about sensitive issues that might be harder to discuss openly. Many NGOs are doing excellent work in prevention and mitigation of the HIV/AIDS epidemic. Their approach may vary: working with high-risk groups or with youths (in and out of school); assisting orphans and needy families; counseling on the impact of HIV/AIDS, including the legal rights of those left behind; or conducting research and instructional activities. However, the government needs to show a strong political will and commitment such that policy and sensitization of HIV/AIDS issues at all levels of the political structure is adequate.

5. TRANSFORMING AGRICULTURE INTO AN ENGINE OF GROWTH AND POVERTY REDUCTION

The sheer size and prominence of agriculture in growth and poverty reduction in Tanzania makes it a focal point for development. Agriculture continues to be the backbone of the Tanzanian economy, currently accounting for about half of the national income and slightly more than half of merchandise exports, and is a source of livelihood for about 80 percent of Tanzanians (see table 5.1). The relatively large share of agriculture in the economy makes the overall growth performance and improvement in the living standards depend greatly on what happens in the sector.

Table 5.1. *Agriculture's Contribution to the National Economy* *(percent)*

Parameter	1970	1975	1980–82	1985–87	1990–92	1997–98
Agriculture share of net exports by value	—	—	90	85	67	51
Agriculture share of GNP	49	45	49	46	45	50
Agriculture share of imports						
Fertilizer	—	—	2	4	4	1
Food	—	—	13	10	3	4
Agriculture share of labor force employment	90	88	86	85	84	82
Population in rural areas	93	90	85	82	79	75

— Not available.
Notes: Agricultural exports are taken as the six main crop exports: cashew, coffee, cotton, sisal, tea, and tobacco. World Bank (1999) estimates that including exports of fish, live animals, horticulture and other nontraditional exports would raise the share of agricultural exports in 1997–98 to 73 percent of total merchandise exports.
Sources: IFPRI and World Bank (2000); World Bank staff estimates.

Agriculture's prominence is further highlighted by the fact that it has large spin-off effects on the nonfarm sector, mainly through forward linkages to agroprocessing and consumption. On the basis of HRDS data, T Sh 1,000 of new household income from export crop sales is estimated to be able to lead to T Sh 2,000 worth of additional local employment in the production of nontradable goods and services. An alternative method for estimating multiplier effects is with a social accounting matrix. Simulations with such a matrix constructed for Tanzania by Wobst (1999) show that this linkage is particularly strong for export agriculture. T Sh 1 worth of income from this source generates T Sh 1.80 increase in overall GDP, in contrast to T Sh 1.20 in response to a similar size stimulus from light manufacturing. Not surprisingly, light manufacturing has a smaller effect on incomes in rural areas, where the vast majority of poverty is. More surprisingly, light manufacturing has a smaller effect on urban incomes than does export cash cropping. This is because light manufacturing is less labor intensive and uses more imports.

Agriculture accounts for half of Tanzanian exports. Furthermore, an analysis of ratios for domestic resource costs reveals that Tanzania has a strong comparative advantage in maize, paddy, and all the traditional export crops. Nontraditional export crops, such as cut flowers, may be highly profitable niche activities, but typically cannot provide the overall employment numbers and consumption linkages compared with the traditional export crops. This is because the nontraditional crops have higher capital requirements, and access to markets for these crops is more difficult. Fisheries offer promise, but are subject to some of the same constraints. Livestock products may offer one of the best long-run potentials in terms of widespread applicability. In any case, the same policy environment that is useful for promoting traditional exports will also be beneficial for promoting nontraditional exports.

Tanzania's overall response to past interventions and reforms are rather unimpressive, judging from the sector's recent performance relative to growth targets for effective poverty reduction. An International Food Policy Research Institute study (IFPRI and World Bank 2000), which reconciles various data sources, estimates that agricultural GDP has grown at 3.3 percent per year since 1985. The six main food crops have grown at 3.5 percent per year, while export crops have grown at 5.4 percent (see table 5.2). Other components, such as livestock and forestry, have lower recorded numbers. Changes in productivity show a stagnant trend. Although this performance is respectable relative to an average African country, it falls far short of the growth Tanzania needs to reduce poverty significantly. The overall growth target would in the range of 6–7 percent if the objective of halving abject poverty by 2010 is to be achieved. Since, in Tanzania, food insecurity is predominantly a problem of low and fluctuating household income rather than merely one of overall availability of food, higher rural incomes hold the answer to improved nutritional standards.

Table 5.2. *Composition of Agricultural Output*

Commodity	Gross domestic product (million T Sh at 1992 prices)	Percentage of agricultural GDP
Crop production	549,569	74.3
Maize	168,492	22.8
Paddy	59,333	8.0
Wheat	3,487	0.5
Millet/Sorghum	33,780	4.6
Cassava	33,602	4.5
Beans	38,673	5.2
Other food crops	144,212	19.5
Cash crops	67,991	9.2
Livestock	98,680	13.3
Forestry, hunting, and fishing	91,691	12.4
Total	739,940	100.0

Source: IFPRI and World Bank (2000).

Progress in reducing poverty, food security, and malnutrition in Tanzania depends greatly on the performance of the agriculture sector for two reasons. First, poverty is primarily a rural phenomenon. The incidence and severity of poverty is twice as high in rural areas as in urban area, urban incomes are 2–3 times greater than rural incomes, and rural households lag behind urban households in almost every indicator of the standard of living. Second, 84 percent of the work force in Tanzania is involved in agricultural production. Even if farmers were not poorer, no development strategy could expect to improve the lives of the majority of the population without significant investment in agriculture.

Econometric analysis of the household data from the HRDS for FY94 (URT 1996) indicates that incomes are substantially lower in rural areas, and within rural areas farmers are poorer than nonfarmers. Among farmers, those who grow cash crops have higher incomes than those who do not, even after farm size, education, and other factors are held constant. Furthermore, increases in income earned by export crop farmers are associated with increased per capita food consumption among this group. Rural households in risky agroclimatic zones or inaccessible areas are most vulnerable to poverty, as they cannot fully benefit from market-oriented reforms because their participation in the market is either extremely limited or highly unstable.

What do trends in poverty and nutrition tell us about the impact of the reforms and the performance of agriculture since 1986? The trends are generally positive or neutral. HRDS data suggest that rural incomes rose and poverty rates fell between 1976 and 1993, the latest year for which data on national household budgets are available. Since the period 1976–84 was one of ever-deepening economic crisis, it is safe to assume that the progress was achieved since the reforms were launched in the mid-1980s. The situation since 1993 is inconclusive because of a lack of consistent information over time, as explained in the previous chapter.

Available evidence indicates that nutrition has either improved or has remained unchanged since the mid-1980s, when the reforms were implemented. Unfortunately, nationally representative nutrition data are only available from the 1991 and 1996 Tanzanian Demographic and Health Surveys. These surveys show a decline in the rate of stunting among children (a measure of chronic malnutrition), while wasting (a measure of recent or acute malnutrition) rose slightly. Nonetheless, the levels of poverty and malnutrition remain high by international standards. Infant mortality is even higher in Zanzibar than in rural areas of the mainland, mostly because access to health care facilities is so poor.

Lessons Learned from Recent Analytic Work

Impact of Reforms

Agriculture has shifted significantly toward a market-oriented environment in the past decade and a half. In the early 1980s, Tanzania was in the midst of a severe economic crisis characterized by 30 percent inflation, unsustainable fiscal and external deficits, shortages of basic consumer goods, the collapse of agricultural exports, and shrinking real income per capita.

Starting in 1984 and accelerating in 1986, the government introduced economic reforms to enable market forces to play a greater role in the economy. From 1986 to 1993, the real exchange rate depreciated significantly, providing better incentives to exporters. Domestic food crop marketing was liberalized, with private traders gradually taking over the role of the cooperatives and crop authorities. From 1991 to 1995, fertilizer subsidies were phased out and markets were opened to private traders. In the mid-1990s, the marketing and export of traditional export crops was liberalized and the commercial role of parastatal crop authorities was scaled back.

Since 1993, however, the real exchange rate has fallen roughly 40 percent. In addition, government expenditure on agriculture has fallen both in absolute real terms and as a percentage of total expenditure. The fiscal savings associated with the elimination of input subsidies and loss-making commercial activities have not been redirected to vital public support for the agriculture sector, even though the participation of the public sector in agriculture may have been scaled back significantly.

The profitability of agriculture has recently declined after a sharp rise in the initial period of reforms. The rise was due to steep depreciation of the shilling and sector policy reforms, and was reversed as a result of sharp real appreciation of the shilling and a slowing down in the pace of reforms. The market-determined producer prices of food in the early 1990s were substantially higher in real terms than the official procurement prices of the 1980s. Interpretation of this difference is complicated, however, because although many farmers sold their harvest on parallel markets even in the 1980s, data for these prices do not exist. In addition, market food prices after 1991 were significantly affected by the 1991–92 drought in southern Africa, which raised prices of maize exports from Tanzania. Real producer prices of food crops have fallen 40–60 percent since 1992 (see table 5.3). These reductions were due to the end of the southern

50

African shortages associated with drought, which had raised product prices for Tanzanian farmers, and to real exchange rate appreciation since 1993. Since 1993, real producer prices for all the principal export crops have fallen between 25 and 70 percent. This has occurred in spite of some reduction in marketing margins due to privatization of marketing and in spite of relatively stable world prices. As a result of the appreciation, the reductions in producer prices for maize, wheat, and rice have been larger (55–60 percent) than those for nontradable crops. A sharp depreciation of the shilling in the second half of 1999 to a large extent clawed back the loss in profitability associated with previous appreciation. A good example is the steep rise in cashew producer prices in the 1999s, which was assisted by increased competition in buying.

Table 5.3. *Real Producer Prices for Food Crops, 1981–99*

Year	Price index[a]	Maize	Paddy	Wheat	Millet	Beans	Cassava
		Crop					
		Official procurement prices (constant FY99 T Sh / kg)					
1981–85	1.4	140	232	195	117	334	—
1986–90	5.6	149	250	170	109	369	—
		Market prices (constant FY99 T Sh / kg)					
FY91	12.3	106	212	473	279	471	—
FY92	14.7	279	370	495	289	508	73
FY93	18.6	298	491	525	365	533	91
FY94	25.2	256	424	497	376	712	84
FY95	32.7	181	254	452	484	797	76
FY96	43.3	165	216	423	538	571	75
FY97	58.3	138	245	362	245	475	67
FY98	77.3	117	195	272	175	431	61
FY99	100.0	118	151	228	175	317	53

— Not available.
a. National Consumer Price Index where FY99 = 100 to April 1999.
Source: IFPRI and World Bank (2000, table 3.1).

World prices influence the producer prices of tradable food crops. To test the tradability of different food crops in Tanzania, monthly retail prices for maize, rice, and cassava were estimated as a function of world prices, the exchange rate, regional supply, national supply, and rainfall. As expected, rice prices throughout Tanzania are strongly influenced by world prices, implying that this crop is tradable. Cassava prices are unaffected by world prices but strongly affected by domestic supply, implying that it is nontradable. Maize prices are affected by world prices in the more accessible regions and by domestic supply alone in the more isolated regions.

Devaluation and input subsidy removal have increased the real price of fertilizer by a factor of 2.5–3.9 over 1991–97. This increase, combined with lower producer prices, has greatly reduced the profitability of fertilizer use—particularly for food crops, such as maize, and particularly in the southern highlands.

An examination of the cost of agricultural marketing using monthly retail food prices in 44 markets shows that marketing margins for maize, rice, and wheat between Dar es Salaam and other cities have narrowed significantly. These changes presumably reflect the increased efficiency of a competitive private sector market and some improvement in marketing infrastructure. However, transfer costs, being in the order of US$0.16 per metric ton per kilometer on the main trade routes, are still too high by international standards. The country's vastness and fringe location of the food basket regions raises the value of investment to bridge the distances and have a more integrated national market.

Lack of Uniform Performance across Crops

Maize production grew at an annual rate of 2.4 percent over 1985–98.This growth rate is slightly less than the population growth rate, but is fairly respectable given the declining real producer price and the large increase in fertilizer prices. The removal of fertilizer subsidies does not seem to be a significant factor in overall productive demand. Effective demand constraints linked to high marketing costs probably play a larger role in limiting maize output growth.

Since 1985, rice output has expanded threefold and wheat production has grown by 60 percent. Both have high income elasticity of demand and are consumed in greater quantities by urban households. An analysis of food demand using HRDS data indicates the estimated income elasticity for maize is relatively low, while the elasticities of wheat, potatoes, animal products, and rice are relatively high. This implies that, as per capita income rises, households will shift from maize and other staples toward more expensive sources of calories. Demand analysis also suggests that urbanization will shift demand away from maize, cassava, and sweet potatoes toward wheat, rice, white potatoes, and animal products. The growth rates of other staple crops tend to track population growth, but have limited demand. Attention needs to be paid to the changing composition of demand as income rises and not just to supply growth of all food crops.

Growth in export-crop production has been strong and robust, except for coffee. Export crop production expanded just 1.8 percent per year during the late 1980s. In contrast, the growth rate in the 1990s was 7.7 percent per year. Strong growth in the production of cashew nuts and tobacco have offset declines in the production of coffee and, more recently, of cotton.

Performance in the important beef cattle sector has been mixed. This is hardly surprising given the long-term fall in domestic and world prices, the rising cost and lower access to veterinary and other livestock services over time, and high and arbitrary levels of local and central taxation. Dairy and poultry have performed well, showing long-term growth rates that are much higher than 4 percent for dairy and probably higher for poultry and eggs. These intensive occupations are overwhelmingly carried out in small operations within city limits. There are anecdotal reports that pork is also expanding in urban areas. This pattern of development implies a continued high rate of growth in concentrated feed use and mounting environmental and public health problems in towns. Animal health also remains an important constraint.

Aggregate data on fisheries are unreliable, but suggest stagnation in aggregate production. Much more reliable data on fishery exports show explosive growth in exports since the mid- to late 1980s. In 1998, Nile perch fillets from Lake Victoria accounted for more than 75 percent of total fisheries exports, which in turn represented more than 8 percent of total merchandise exports, up from a negligible amount in the mid-1980s.

Principal Constraints to the Development of Agriculture

Agriculture in Tanzania has been severely discriminated against in the past by urban-oriented policies. It is only now beginning to regain some vitality in the key export sectors, despite heavy taxation; high transport costs; and, more recently, unfavorable movements in the real exchange rate. To a large extent the basic constraints faced by both smallholder and "commercial" farmers are similar in nature. The main differences between the two are related to the "marketing" issues, which the latter face (in addition to employment issues); these are international trade-related and taxation bottlenecks.

Intensification

Constrained access to inputs and timely advice, to a large extent, holds back progress in the intensification of agriculture. Indeed agricultural research and extension generate high returns on investment, as demonstrated by hundreds of rate of return studies. Furthermore a study of India, the details of which are provided below, indicates government spending on research and development (R&D) ranked as the most effective for raising productivity growth in agriculture. This observation serves as a reference point for the preparation of R&D. The problems of R&D in Tanzania mainly relate to poor transfer of knowledge from research to application, erratic access to extension agents, and the more recent transitional problems from decentralizing the management of extension services to the local governments. These problems are particularly acute for smallholder crops, such as cotton, food crops, and coffee, in contrast to crops such as tea and sisal, where big farmers or marketing and processing companies finance research, provide the bulk of extension services, or both.

The use of fertilizer has fallen by about half as a result of subsidies being removed and of lower crop prices. However, the impact on production of fertilizer-using crops has been negligible, suggesting either inadequate application or wastage in use. This is not to underrate the potential impact of intensification, but to call attention to complementary measures needed for effectiveness. In the case of export crops, such as tobacco and coffee, fertilizer remains profitable in many cases, but use may be constrained by lack of credit.

Farmers' responsiveness to price incentives in Tanzania has been confirmed by econometric analysis using annual regional panel data for both food and export crop production. The main constraints to commercialization relate to the unavailability of price information, wide marketing margins resulting from poor infrastructure, and weak competition in markets. In 1992 the marketing margins were, on average, 48 percent of f.o.b. prices for exported crops and 25 percent for domestic sales, the difference being explained by the longer distances covered to the export points. Furthermore, costs are associated with restrictions to crop movements, and excessive taxes and their inconsistent application across local governments. Concerns have also been raised regarding restrictions of access to regional markets in the case of food crops, which hamper producers in the border areas from making the most profitable sales.

Commercialization

Improving marketing infrastructure is essential for increased productivity, because this enables a more efficient flow of larger volumes of produce and raises the profitability of agriculture through reducing marketing costs. With the dismantling of public monopolies in agricultural marketing, the excessive margins exacted from producers have declined. This decline has made transport costs the highest cost element in marketing. Private marketing agents are emerging, but rather slowly, and are confining themselves to more accessible areas in terms of transport. Thus improvement in transport infrastructure is needed to ensure wide coverage of marketing services and to ensure that marketing agents are not starved of required credit for their operations.

Agricultural Credit

Formal credit for agricultural marketing has experienced a spectacular collapse in the past five years. Commercial bank lending has been increasing overall, but the share of loans for agricultural marketing fell from 19.7 percent of the total in 1995 to a mere 0.8 percent in 1999. The sharp drop by two-thirds between 1995 and 1996 is associated with a lending freeze by the National Bank of Commerce, enforced under the memorandum of understanding with the treasury in the context of the restructuring of the bank.

Availability of formal agricultural credit for production is limited. Just 5 percent of Tanzanian farmers obtain credit from nonfamily sources in a given year, the main constraint to credit expansion being risks associated with poor recovery of credit. Commercial bank lending for agricultural production has halved in the past four years, declining from a peak of nearly 12 percent of total domestic lending in 1996 to 6 percent in 1999. Although for food crops, such as maize, the profitability of inputs is a problem, in the case of export crops, fertilizer is more often profitable and probably underused.

The bulk of the rural economy depends to a large extent on informal credit arrangements. These are typically small and segmented and cannot typically meet investment financing needs. In the past, public credit schemes and development banks attempted to fill this gap. However, in the wake of the termination of the cooperatives and the Cooperatives and Rural Development Bank, which then were the main channels for rural credit, all such institutions have now ended their lending activities. The existing banking system, which is increasingly privatized, caters mostly to large clients and offers short-term credit. Prospectively only the National Microfinance Bank is expected to play the role of availing credit through microfinance programs. Nongovernmental agencies, such as PRIDE, have been channeling resources from donors and the Tanzania Gender Networking Program, and the government has set up specific funds to offer credit to communities and individuals. However, there is still a serious shortage of long-term microfinance for smallholders who are seeking resources for investment.

A variety of experiments are under way to develop rules and institutions to facilitate input credit for export crop producers, including strengthened contractual arrangements with marketing agents and credit to self-selected groups within villages who guarantee their members in securing credit from third parties. These groups are typically registered entities with bank accounts they own and manage themselves. The main problem with the current contractual credit arrangement between farmers and the marketing and processing companies is how to ensure credit recovery in a liberalized market, where farmers have various market outlets.

Government Investment Effectiveness

A recent study analyzed the relative effectiveness of different categories of government spending aimed at reducing rural poverty and promoting productivity growth in India. The results of the study indicated public spending on roads to be the most effective factor in reducing poverty, largely through raising rural incomes, and was second only to research and development in raising productivity growth. A similar impact assessment done through simulation for Tanzania by Wobst (1999) concluded that rural farm households with low incomes and that are not oriented toward producing export crops benefit most from better infrastructure. Spending on education, but not health, had a small but significant impact on both poverty and productivity growth in agriculture. These assessments suggest that the government should focus its spending on sectors with the most potential impact on productivity growth and rural poverty reduction: infrastructure and education.

Four key constraints hamper the development of the private sector in agriculture. One is credit, which was dealt with earlier in this memorandum. The second is the unpredictable imposition of controls for internal and external movement of agricultural produce, which hampers marketing efficiency and profitability of

54

agriculture. The third concerns taxes: the large number of taxes and charges levied on agriculture, the lack of reasonable uniformity in treatment across localities, and the multiple taxation at different levels of government. Fourth is a lack of a unified and organized voice to clearly articulate the concerns of private sector interests to small and large farmers through government policies and private sector lobbies.

Institutional Framework for Rural Development

The government made most of the policy interventions in the sector (addressing organization and techniques of production for fostering growth of agricultural output) in great part by looking at the sector in relation to itself, only marginally taking into account the strong relationship between agriculture and other sectors. Yet it is a well established fact that the performance of agriculture hinges on what happens outside the sector itself, particularly in infrastructure, finance, and human capital (education and health) development. Furthermore, public sector withdrawal from commercial activities in agriculture in the last decade has left critical gaps in supportive services, particularly in input distribution, quality control, and credit. These gaps have yet to be filled by the private sector.

The lack of clearly defined and coordinated responsibilities among the various Tanzanian government institutions for the development of agriculture and rural development more broadly has constrained the development of a coherent strategy for the transformation of agriculture. As a result, actions have tended to be disparate and often reactive in nature. The Ministry of Agriculture and Cooperatives has not been able to galvanize and coordinate the wide range of interventions by the Prime Minister's Office, the Ministry of Regional Administration and Local Government, and the Ministry of Finance with those of its own in supporting the predominantly private sector and NGO activities in agriculture. The situation is made more complex by the absence of a sectorwide framework and cross-sector coordination mechanisms for the transformation of agriculture in the context of a rural development strategy. Such mechanisms need to recognize the wide diversity of the needs of the different subsectors, agroclimatic zones, and rural communities. This is probably the key challenge for the government in the immediate future.

Key Elements of a Cohesive Strategy

Long-Term Strategy

A cohesive long-term strategy for agriculture-led growth in Tanzania involves at least five central elements:

- Sustained macroeconomic stability.
- More effective research and extension.
- Improved infrastructure.
- A tax and regulatory environment that is conducive to investment by both enterprise and individual farmers.
- A coherent institutional framework for supporting the transformation of agriculture and rural development more broadly.

From the evidence presented earlier, what seems to matter for improved performance of agriculture to a large extent depends on what happens outside the institutions directly responsible for agriculture. While, within the sector, research and extension have been singled out as most potent for both productivity growth and poverty reduction, outside the sector better roads and education, increased access to finance, lower and more transparent taxation, and greater contestability of markets are all critical for success. The question is, what is an appropriate institutional arrangement or instrument for pulling these together in a cohesive strategy? A rural development strategy under the TAS is a useful starting point, and the MTEF can serve as a coordinating resource allocation instrument. The institutional framework for implementing and monitoring such a strategy, however, will require some reorganization that takes into account the increased involvement of local governments, community organizations, and NGOs in a decentralized approach. Institutional arrangements must be designed that can ensure effective intersectoral coordination without at the same time being intrusive on private sector involvement in the agriculture sector.

SUSTAINED MACROECONOMIC STABILITY. While the government has been successful in maintaining a stable macroeconomic environment for the past five years, one worrisome outcome was the renewed sharp appreciation of the real exchange rate between 1993 and mid-1999, which eroded the profitability and competitiveness of Tanzanian agriculture. The long-term solution for minimizing such erosion is to ensure that Tanzania's inflation is close to par with that of its trading partners, so as to minimize incipient real appreciation when Tanzanian inflation exceeds that of its partners. In the short term, however, the effects from changes in fundamentals, including surges in capital inflows, may have to be managed prudently through open-market operations by the Bank of Tanzania, observing limitations in the capacity to intervene effectively. The government should be cautioned, however, not to repoliticize the exchange rate by avoiding direct interventions to change the value of the local currency.

INVESTMENT IN RESEARCH AND EXTENSION. Agricultural research and extension in Tanzania is being carried out by both the government and the private sector. The private sector's involvement is a recent phenomenon and is largely confined to commercial crops, such as tea. Relying entirely on private-sector research is not an option, because of externalities, and because coverage of smallholder crops must be ensured. In the case of export crops and tradable food crops, almost all the benefits of research accrue to farmers, because prices are set by world markets. In the case of nontradable food crops, productivity-increasing research is likely to lower market prices, with benefits shared between producers and consumers.

Facilitating the adoption of technological innovations for raising both land and labor productivity is key for success. Agricultural research for adapting imported technology and improved seeds to local conditions, as well as developing new varieties and technology is one part of this effort. To this end, the decline in agricultural research support must be reversed and ways of rationalizing research on a regional scale for similar ecological conditions must be found. National and regional research infrastructure exists but is underfunded. A related aspect in technological diffusion is the creation of an effective system for conveying new technological information. The vast improvement in media can be harnessed for this purpose, and curricula in the education system can be used to infuse knowledge on best practices.

However, development of a sharper prioritization of research that is demand driven is also needed. Furthermore, support for research should carefully balance national programs (mainly those that are crop specific) and locational programs (for example, for viable technologies) under the decentralization system. For the latter, the matching-grant approach being piloted in the area around Lake Victoria could be considered. The Ministry of Agriculture and Cooperatives' oversight for peer review and for enabling exchange of knowledge nationally and internationally in a network fashion would be important.

The agricultural extension system has not been spared from the budgetary crunch in the last decade and a half. The lack of funding has affected the quality of extension agents and the extent of geographic area their services cover. Strengthening capacity for extension services, therefore, requires better training of agents, improved access to new information on available technology and husbandry, and provision of facilities to reach farmers on a more regular basis. The basic principles should be demand-driven provision of extension services and accommodation of a wide range of providers and needs. Again, coordination should be ensured among the various parties, nationally by the Ministry of Agriculture and Cooperatives and locally by local governments. The professional capacity of district management for coordinating these activities is weak, and the ministry has a key role in ensuring their improvement and effectiveness. Where mixed farming is practiced, livestock extension personnel who are better trained need to be integrated with crop extension services. Otherwise, specialized services need to be provided to pastoralists and those engaged in intensive livestock systems (for example, dairy) particularly in peri-urban areas. In addition, for the extension services to be effectively demand driven, information on improved husbandry and technology must be widely disseminated.

A closer link between research systems and extension services will enable a more effective flow of information between the two agents of innovation. Diffusion of information on technological innovation can be furthered by raising the capacity of farmers to absorb and apply new technology and varieties, and improved husbandry, as availed by the extension system. Education is an important part of this capability. There is evidence that farm productivity improves with primary education through farmers' enhanced ability to access information on innovations and to apply it correctly. The largest impact has been from primary education (Appleton and Balihuta 1996), which is consistent with our earlier remark that budgetary support should be refocused toward primary and secondary education.

INVESTMENT IN RURAL INFRASTRUCTURE. Transportation costs are a large share of the cost of agricultural marketing in Tanzania. Improved roads and better rail service would raise the producer price of export crops, reduce the farm-level cost of fertilizer and other inputs, and reduce spatial margins in food marketing. It would also allow more rural Tanzanian households to earn income from commercialized agriculture. Currently the rural road network (which consists of rural and feeder roads) is allocated about 60 percent of the Road Fund (30 percent through the Ministry of Regional Administration and Local Government and another 30 percent through the ministry and TANROADS in the future). Given the high effectiveness of expenditure on roads in enhancing productivity and commercialization of agriculture, funding beyond the provision under the Road Fund should be considered.

The improvement of the rural road network entails establishing links between villages and markets to enhance commercialization and access to inputs as well as intracommunity links. For the latter, involving the rural communities in identifying needs and maintaining the network is key for sustainability. Support from the districts should be essentially technical, and better-quality advice is needed in this regard. The Village Travel and Transport Project is an interesting pilot, as the initiatives implemented under it are community driven and focus also on reducing the drudgery of labor by helping to reduce distances to essential services. This approach is particularly helpful in reducing the excessive burden borne by women and girls in household chores and family activities.

Similarly, expansion of the phone network (landline or wireless), improved access to newspapers, and increased radio ownership would facilitate spatial arbitrage and market integration through better access to information.

ADDING VALUE TO PRODUCTS AND OFF-FARM INCOME GENERATION. To help diversify income sources in rural areas and minimize risks, a rural development strategy could promote agriculture-related enterprise in rural areas. The potential range of activities include agricultural services, input supply, small-scale agricultural processing, seed multiplication, fish farming, and a range of dairy products. A combination of financial support and extension services for microenterprise would spur the setting up and growth of enterprise activities in the rural areas, leading to better and more accessible services as well as diversifying sources of income.

GOOD GOVERNANCE. The incentives for investing are affected not just by formal regulations and codified tax policy, but also by intangible aspects of governance, such as the attitude of public officials toward the private sector, the certainty and continuity of the business environment, and the risk of exposure to corruption. Broadly speaking, six key areas of action are proposed as focal points for improving the business environment in agriculture. One is removal of controls for internal movement of agricultural produce, to enable greater marketing efficiency and to remove artificial shortages. The second is reduction in the number of taxes and charges levied on agriculture. The third is the encouragement of reasonable uniformity of treatment across localities to improve predictability for potential investors and the removal of multiple taxation at different levels of government to foster greater transparency. The fourth area of action is conversion of the crop boards to being stakeholder entities, with justification for their existence being closely linked to the benefits accruing to farmers who finance crop board activities through crop cess. Fifth is the development and clear articulation of action plans. Such plans would strengthen a unified voice for private sector interests across small and large farmers and resolve any conflicts of interest across these two groups. They would also serve to strengthen the dialogue between the government and the private sector. Finally, a decision needs to be made on the appropriate regulatory framework for a more liberal operation of the sector following the conclusion of studies and consultations on this matter. Although decisions to institute some of these measures have been made in principle, action in these areas needs to be galvanized. Some of these measures can be implemented in the short to medium term and are taken up in greater detail later.

Under the local government reform program, extension, veterinary, and some R&D services, as well as regulatory functions, will be decentralized. Therefore, delineation of the roles for the Ministry of Agriculture and Cooperatives, local governments, community and farmer organizations, and NGOs in the delivery of these services at this level is needed. A crucial aspect for effective decentralization is the managerial capacity of local governments to ensure good plans, coordination, and financial accountability.

Short- to Medium-Term Strategy

The government can implement several measures to stimulate agriculture and boost rural standards of living in Tanzania in the short to medium term. They include limiting local taxation of agriculture, liberalizing regional food trade, promoting agricultural credit, reexamining the impact of food aid, improving data collection and analytical capacity, and increasing budgetary support for agriculture. The effectiveness of these measures would be further increased if they were introduced as a package for revitalizing agriculture, since they would serve as a public signal of the government's commitment to address the problem of rural poverty and the low returns to agriculture.

IMPROVING THE AFFORDABILITY, AVAILABILITY, AND QUALITY OF AGRICULTURAL INPUTS. Pursuit of productivity growth in agriculture is critical for raising returns to applied or committed resources. This effort would require several critical interventions. These are in addition to the consolidation of the realignment of price incentives, which have been implemented for the past decade and a half, and to the reduction of the gross, burdensome taxation of agriculture through reforms. These interventions should help create conditions that are conducive to long-term investment for improving the productivity of the main agricultural resources, land and labor. Existing land tenure arrangements do not attract longer-term commitment of resources for improving productivity of land, including drainage and irrigation. The new land law (enacted February 1999) has provided a foundation for a more transparent execution of land-based transactions and property rights. However, the administrative procedures still have problems that need to be addressed, as well as in the use of land as collateral for obtaining credit. The pace in providing permanent occupancy titles has typically been slow, and the system of allocation is still fraught with corrupt practices. The weak administrative capacity of village governments to apply the law within the decentralized system of land administration is also worrisome. This situation introduces significant uncertainties that militate against long-term investment and encourage the "mining" of soil nutrients. Raising the capacity of the concerned institutions for surveying land and issuing titles to holders is the first important step. Preservation of these rights against the risk of expropriation and the ability to settle disputes fairly and expeditiously are important components of establishing firm property rights.

The private market for agricultural inputs is slowly getting established, albeit with some teething problems. The use of contractual arrangements, where crop buyers supply inputs on credit that are to be recovered when the crops are sold, seems to be working reasonably well for tobacco. These arrangements are supplemented by support from crop boards. The main strategy should revolve around more cost-effectiveness in the sourcing and distribution of inputs, such as fertilizers and chemicals. Furthermore, the emergence of private, local sellers of inputs needs to be supported, and the contractual arrangements for input supply need to be strengthened. While the production of breeder seeds will continue to take place in research stations, breeder seed farms can be commercialized in various localities. Support for the establishment of small, private traders for agricultural inputs should be essentially in the form of improving the business environment. It is, however, important to support skill enhancement for running businesses, and appropriate extension services can be used to provide pertinent advice.

PROMOTING AGRICULTURAL CREDIT. Initiatives are under way to strengthen the microfinance system in the country, and the policy governing its operation has been approved. The process of setting up the microfinance bank to cater to small, rural investors, among others, has benefited from lessons of successful experiences in Asia (for example, the Grameen Bank). Self-selecting groups within villages have also organized themselves as credit unions and guarantee members' credit applications. The success of these schemes is crucial for supporting agricultural investment. It is not just a matter of mobilizing financial resources but, more important, of providing knowledge about investing, which will ensure minimal default in repayments through good selection of investments, and providing mechanisms for enforcing repayments. These would supplement existing social networks engaged in informal credit arrangements that operate on the basis of social trust and sanctions against defaulters.

The government should encourage and facilitate systems for providing input credit to farmers. The system will be more sustainable if credit is provided by crop buyers, banks, and cooperatives rather than by the government; interest rates are not subsidized; and the system targets producers of commercial crops for which inputs are profitable. The government can facilitate credit systems by making repayment easier to enforce, by facilitating the creation of groups for group lending schemes, and by generating information on the returns to input use. It can also mediate between buyers and growers to create loan recovery systems that are transparent and enforceable, particularly in the case of export crops. The bulk of credit needs for rural households are met through informal credit arrangements. Attention to these arrangements has been miniscule, despite their key role in meeting the needs of the rural community. Similarly, farm-related investments have most often been financed through farmers' own savings. Thus, while rural microfinance policy and institutions are being developed to enhance access to formal credit, ways must be found to promote informal credit arrangements and to facilitate increased investment by households in agriculture.

LIMITING LOCAL TAXATION OF AGRICULTURE. The central government must take a role in preventing excessive or arbitrary taxation of agricultural production and marketing by local authorities. The decentralization of revenue generation and agricultural support services has led to different tax regimes being applied in different districts, and also apparently to some arbitrary differences within districts. Agriculture, particularly export agriculture, is an easy target for local revenue collection but should not carry more than its share of local government budgets. The 1999 Finance Bill has gone a long way toward streamlining agricultural taxation and has set ceilings for charges. The main issue now is enforcing compliance to these orders.

LIBERALIZING REGIONAL FOOD TRADE. The government should consider permanently lifting the ban on food exports. This would assist farmers in the border regions, particularly those in the southern highlands near Zambia. The effect of export liberalization on poor consumers in deficit areas would be minor and could be offset by direct assistance. It is difficult to justify having poor farmers "pay" for assistance to maize consumers, many of whom are relatively well off. Similarly, the government should adopt and enforce a clear policy banning restrictions or taxation of agricultural trade within Tanzania.

REEXAMINING THE IMPACT OF FOOD AID. Food aid is essential for addressing temporary shortages and hunger, but it can also make food markets less predictable and lower returns to farmers. Since the poor are primarily food farmers, it is questionable whether regular annual food aid is really serving the interests of equity. Food aid should be temporary and well targeted, and should be used sparingly. Domestically, identifying agroclimatic zones with high weather-related risk will assist in the design of special interventions for risk management, including irrigation. Availability of reliable information about the food market will limit unnecessary emergency interventions by both the public institutions and the private sector.

IMPROVING DATA COLLECTION AND ANALYTICAL CAPACITY. The implementation of survey-based estimates of agricultural production is a step forward, but other data gaps need to be addressed. Better or more recent information is needed on the production of horticulture and other "minor" crops, the use of fertilizer and other inputs, food consumption patterns, the geographic distribution of poverty, interregional marketing flows, and trends in nutrition. Some survey work and analysis could be contracted to local consultants, such as the Economic Research Bureau of the University of Dar es Salaam. Unencumbered access to such data will facilitate analysis and design of solutions for emerging problems on a timely basis.

INCREASING BUDGETARY SUPPORT FOR AGRICULTURE. Correct assessment of the adequacy of government support given to agriculture requires analyzing the option of consolidating budgetary support for agriculture across sectors and levels of government. This should then form the basis for raising support to the sector. Budgetary support is particularly important in the areas of agricultural research and extension, rural infrastructure, and data collection. Even if donor support is forthcoming, local funding is vital for establishing sustainable programs that reflect government priorities.

6. PRIVATE SECTOR DEVELOPMENT

Throughout the postindependence period, the private sector has been the most dominant contributor to the livelihood, growth, and limited dynamism of the Tanzanian economy. On average, the sector has accounted for more than 70 percent of GDP and more than 60 percent of fixed investment. More recently, the private sector has dominated the rehabilitation of the ailing industrial sector, mainly through the privatization program; expansion of the export base; and investment in mining and tourism, which are currently the most dynamic sectors. With the liberalization of trade and the rolling back of the public sector's involvement in commerce, the private sector is also consolidating its dominant role in commerce. The private sector is increasingly strengthening its participation in the direct provision of social services—education and health—particularly since the second half of the 1980s. Previously these services were essentially the exclusive preserve of the government. In this last respect, the private sector seems to be moving toward dominating the supply of social services at the secondary and tertiary levels, while the public sector plays an overwhelmingly dominant role in the provision of these services at the primary level.

In spite of the recent significant improvements, one of the less impressive outcomes of reforms has been the rather weak response of private sector investment to the measures taken so far. Private investment as a proportion of GDP remains at 12 percent, which is low even by African standards. Without a robust investment response, the productive capacity of the economy will remain stagnant and growth cannot rise or be sustained. A good part of the recorded investment during the past decade has been rehabilitative in nature and hardly keeps up with the continued decommissioning of public enterprise capacity, as these get weaned off budgetary subventions. Part of the foreign investment outside mining and tourism has financed transfer of ownership in the privatization process rather than added capacity.

Measures must therefore be taken to encourage a more robust response of private investment in Tanzania and increased productivity of investment. Such investment response needs also to be broadly distributed across sectors in contrast to the recent concentration in the enclave sectors of mining and tourism. Spreading income-earning opportunities to reach the poor entails encouraging investment in smallholder agriculture as well as in small and medium enterprises. The effort must therefore be directed not only at raising the overall level of private investment but also at paying attention to its poverty-reducing quality through a broad distribution of investor response across sectors.

Lessons from the Past

The private sector's prominence in the economy has experienced a checkered history, depending largely on the government's stance toward its own role in the economy relative to that of the private sector. Three main phases can be identified during which the private sector's role has declined sharply: a dominant position at independence, a virtual struggle for survival over the next two decades, and a rapid revival in the 1990s. In the process, Tanzania lost two decades of private sector development, and indeed, its potential contribution to overall development. This loss is also manifested in the current infancy of entrepreneurship among indigenous Tanzanians and weaknesses in institutions that are charged with the responsibility of effectively governing the execution of private business and property rights. The evolution of the policy environment had a profound influence on the space created for private sector initiative, the incentive structure affecting the profitability of private ventures, the openness and competitiveness of the environment in which the sector operates, and the institutional framework governing risk perceptions and security of property.

Phase 1: 1961–68

In the early postindependence period, 1961–68, the government played a supportive role to the private sector. This phase was characterized by macroeconomic stability and a capital-friendly environment conducive to the development of the private sector. Much as the institutional structure was nascent and fragile, the stance the government adopted toward the private sector then was relatively nonintrusive and broadly favored foreign participation in a broad range of sectors. The protective walls for the domestic industry were still diminutive.

Aware of the importance of other development actors in the implementation of the First Five-Year Plan, the government institutionalized two main consultative bodies: the Sectoral Relations Committee and the National Economic and Social Council. The committee was composed of representatives from the private sector and relevant sectoral ministries of the government. It facilitated communication between the private sector and the government on the development of and problems faced by the sector. The council was a forum for interaction between the government and representatives of the various professional and social communities on the various aspects of the plan. These two bodies provided an opportunity for the various stakeholders in the development process to interact with the government on the achievements, constraints and prospects of the plan.

Phase 2: 1969–85

The second phase saw a significant shift toward a dirigist and socialist strategy. The main objective was to establish the dominant position of the public sector in the commanding heights of the economy, built around socialist principles. In addition to the traditional functions of providing economic and social infrastructure, as well as maintaining law and order, the public sector drove into the commercial activities spanning production and commerce. The policy thrust of the Arusha Declaration placed the responsibility for investment on the government. Thus, in the Second Five-Year Plan, and later in the Third Five-Year Plan, the government development budget was to be the main source of investment, including subventions to parastatal and cooperative investment programs. Comparatively, private sector investment was forecasted to grow at a much slower rate, with a share in investment not to exceed 12 percent as a matter of policy. This limiting of the private sector's share in investment indicated the deliberate strategy of diminishing its importance in total investment in the economy. Furthermore, private investment was to be largely confined to a narrow range of activities: residential construction, transport equipment, large construction projects, and the production of miscellaneous manufacturing and agricultural equipment.

Private enterprise survived a difficult period of controls during the 1970s and a good part of the 1980s, to a large extent through use of the informal financial system and the growth of parallel markets in contravention to these restrictions. The collapse of private investment during this period, from an average share of more than 60 percent in the early 1960s to less than 40 percent through the 1980s, nevertheless manifested the difficulties the sector faced under this restrictive system. In a more fundamental sense, this was a period of perverse development of the private sector. Private ventures that developed during this period did so under a pervasive rent-seeking environment and largely depended on protection by the state and on preferential access to state-controlled resources. The mindset was therefore tuned to connections with those in control to get ahead and survive. Thus the incentive structure was loaded against the development of an efficient private sector, and further reinforced rent-seeking that the country is now struggling to undo. Business capabilities and supportive skills of the labor force also remained relatively undeveloped.

Phase 3: 1986–Present

During the second half of the 1980s and all of the 1990s, the government made several policy and institutional changes that had a positive bearing on private sector development. Although structural reforms and removal of gross price distortions began in the second half of the 1980s, it was not until the early 1990s that these measures found a firm footing in institutional and legal terms. The foreign exchange market was liberalized, exchange controls were dismantled, the financial market was opened up to private sector participation, and the privatization process was formally launched. The second half of the 1990s saw an acceleration of the freeing up of markets, sustained improvements in the macroeconomic stability, acceleration in the pace of privatization, further freeing up of markets, and proactive encouragement of foreign investment. The government promulgated the National Investment Promotion Policy and enacted the National Investment (Promotion and Protection) Act, 1990. The act established the Investment Promotion Center, spelled out priority sectors for investment by local and foreign investors, and guaranteed investment protection. Realizing the inherent deficiencies in the new law, the government amended the Tanzania Investment Act, 1997, to make the Tanzania Investment Center a one-stop center for investors in coordinating, encouraging, promoting, and facilitating investment in Tanzania.

The private sector response to these changes has been cautious but overall positive, as is evident in the rapid rise of its share in investment and output: 21 private banks now account for nearly 50 percent of total assets in the banking system, if NBC(1997) is included. Under Amalgamated Banks of South Africa, the share of assets will most likely rise to nearly 80 percent. The share of fixed investment in the private sector rose to nearly 80 percent and that of net output to 99 percent. FDI rose from US$20 million in 1994 to US$165 million in 1998. Public monopoly in the financial sector has ended. The insurance market has been opened up to private and foreign participation, and a stock exchange is now operational. The infrastructure sector is increasingly coming under the private sector through privatization, turning the management of assets over to private operators, and through entry of new infrastructure components. This cuts across railways, power, communications, and shipping services. The most robust response has been in the mining and tourism sectors, the destination of the bulk of foreign investment.

As the private sector revives, important transitional issues must be considered. Many old businesses (the average age of industrial enterprises is estimated at 17.5 years), which were built with the Tanzanian government as the primary client or source of subsidized resources, may prove to be unsustainable if they do not undertake significant structural reforms. This is particularly the case as the government is downsizing its involvement and spinning off functions to private providers. Those firms, which were established on the premise that the government would maintain high protective walls, may similarly have to survive more open and intensive co7mpetition. The continued positive output growth in all sectors indicates that some older firms have already proved to be capable of handling this pressure. The new generation of firms established under the new dispensation had to contend with these realities right from the start. What appears to be emerging is that the surviving older firms and the new firms have more than covered for losses from firms folding up. This sets up the basis for a much more efficient and robust private sector.

Constraints to Private Sector Development

Instability of the Macroeconomic Environment

The stability of the macroeconomic environment and the efficiency of markets influence business expectations and operative costs. Much as significant success has been made in stabilizing the economy and removing most gross policy distortions, concern now needs to turn to sustaining this positive environment and removing the underlying pressures to avoid possible reversals. Concerns about the risks of policy reversals can only be dealt with if measures are taken to bind the various positive policy changes through legal provisions and institutional arrangements, which cannot so easily be reversed. This process is still at an early stage and is fraught with obstacles related to difficulties in changing mindsets, vested interests, the political hurdles to proceeding expeditiously and resolutely, and capacity constraints for designing and implementing the required changes.

Movement of the exchange rate has engendered concerns from both exporters (when it appreciates) and importers (when it depreciates). The government has typically desisted from intervening to influence the level of exchange rate, given that Tanzania has chosen the path of a monetary approach to stabilization and has left the exchange rate to be market determined. This choice is probably the best, given the limitations of various intervention options. Large interventions through open market operations in the foreign exchange market are hardly tenable, given the limited size of the reserves under the Bank of Tanzania. Experience from other countries with more reserves (Kenya and Zimbabwe) has shown that this option was unworkable against a significant currency slide prompted by changes in fundamentals and proved to be disastrous to the reserve position. A sustainable approach is to bring down inflation to the level of Tanzania's principal trading partners, which would minimize the pressure for depreciation and thus reestablish the parity of purchasing power with trading partners. This approach has two advantages. First, it ensures that the exchange rate does not appreciate on the basis of purchasing power parity (judging from continued positive output growth in all sectors). Second, it keeps away government intervention, and therefore political pressure on the exchange rate. The approach ought to be supplemented by judicious sterilization of capital flows and booms in export earnings, which generate pressure on the local currency to appreciate.

Although some progress has been made in reforming and liberalizing the financial sector, the provision of financial services still has a number of weaknesses and deficiencies. One is the continuing fragmentation of the financial market. Competition in the sector also remains weak, as reflected by the wide spread between borrowing and lending rates in banks. Real deposit rates currently average 3 percent, while real lending rates are nearly 13 percent. Large overdrafts and nonperforming commercial bank assets endanger the solvency of the banking system and are now being eliminated. Commercial banking activities—mainly financing trade-related activities—continue to be highly concentrated in urban centers, while agriculture remains starved of credit. This credit starvation hampers the development of the sector payment and clearing system, which remains inefficient. The gaps left behind following the folding-up of development banks have not been filled by the private sector. The capital market remains shallow and weak, with low liquidity. These weaknesses will have to be addressed if a robust response from private investors to is be expected. The deepening of the reforms and continued privatization in the sector is expected eventually to foster higher competition and efficiency.

Administrative and Institutional Impediments to Business Operation and Investment

A number of private investor surveys and assessments point to weaknesses in taxation policy and tax administration as among the key factors that muffle the investment response from the private sector. Examples of the foregoing include tariff barriers to unencumbered foreign trade; nuisance taxes at various levels of governments, which hamper new investment and expansion of old business; and nontax barriers to the internal and external flow of goods.

Foremost among the administrative constraints are bureaucratic red tape faced by investors and exporters, deficiencies in the legal framework, weak enforcement of property rights, and corruption. Nontransparent policies and laws governing property ownership, labor and immigration laws that hamper mobility of labor, and lack of mechanisms for expeditious settlement of commercial disputes in a fair and transparent way compound the challenges faced by private investors. Such impediments are perhaps key in constraining trade and require strong resolve if the government is to pursue institutional restructuring and a virtual overhaul of competencies and attitudes. The legal framework has largely lagged behind the process of reforms and can hardly support the requirements of the market-oriented economy. The judiciary capacity similarly is weak and needs to be retuned to the commercial orientation of the economy. In this respect, the lack of appropriate public sector incentives for attracting and retaining a well-qualified and motivated cadre of legal experts is a serious issue.

Business risks include policy risk (risk of reversals), sovereign risk (expropriation and default), and risks associated with political instability (safety of property). The main uncertainty about reforms would be lingering attitudes in the public service that are unfriendly toward the private sector, inertia of the control economy, and vested interests or protectionist stances of those elements in the private sector that cannot effectively make the transition to the more open and liberalized environment. Actions for binding and securing the reforms against reversals should thus be the main focus here.

Constraints to Competitiveness

Some constraints have a direct bearing on the competitiveness of the business sector and greater contestability in markets, which are needed to spur efficiency in business through competition and to ensure a level playing field. These include the absence of well-articulated regulatory frameworks to govern a transparent and fair operation of markets, trade barriers raising the cost of imports to local businesses, higher cost of finance, higher taxation, and poor availability and higher cost of infrastructure services.

According to the *Africa Competitiveness Report* (World Economic Forum and Center for International Development 2000), for the period 1996–99 Tanzania has improved its overall rank in competitiveness to 14 (out of a cohort of 24 countries), moving to the first rank in the "improvement" index category while maintaining a rank of second in the "optimism" index. As the liberalization process gathers momentum, strengthening of the regulatory framework in key markets is strongly needed to enhance transparency in the business environment and to increase competition. This needs to be pursued at the same time forbearance of unwanted business practices that spawn inefficiency is avoided. The liberalization process entails:

- Enacting laws that govern a transparent regulatory framework for the key supportive sectors, such as utilities, petroleum, finance, and other infrastructure.
- Setting up institutions for administering the regulatory frameworks.
- Providing appropriate adjudication machinery within the commercial court framework to deal with disputes that may arise in connection with applying the relevant laws.

Studies on appropriate regulatory frameworks are almost completed that cover a large range of specific sectors and options for setting up the required institutional structures. A consultative process is being proposed to help determine the most appropriate regulatory framework to be applied, including a rationalization in the setup across sectors to minimize costs associated with this function. What will be needed is an expeditious adoption of agreed on frameworks for implementing and operationalizing the institutions for dealing with the many complaints that are bound to come from providers and users of these services regarding lack of fairness and deterioration in service delivery.

The obstacles to private sector development in Tanzania are compared with those in other countries in the region in table 6.1

Table 6.1. *Reported Obstacles to Doing Business in Selected Sub-Saharan Africa Countries, Total Number and Ranking*

Ranking of obstacles	Kenya	Tanzania	Uganda	Malawi	Mauritius	Madagascar
Unpredictability of the judiciary	—	—	—	—	—	1
Regulations for starting business/new operations	—	—	—	—	—	—
Price controls	—	—	—	—	—	—
Regulations on foreign trade (exports, imports)	—	—	—	—	—	—
Financing	5	3	3	—	—	8
Labor regulations	—	—	—	—	—	—
Foreign currency regulations	—	—	—	—	—	—
Tax regulations and/or high taxes	4	1	1	—	—	1
Inadequate supply of infrastructure	1	2	—	1	—	5
Policy instability	—	—	—	—	—	4
Safety or environmental regulations	—	—	—	—	—	—
Inflation	—	5	—	3	—	6
General uncertainty on costs of regulations	—	—	—	—	—	—
Crime and theft	2	—	—	2	—	7
Corruption	2	4	2	—	—	3
Terrorism	—	—	—	—	—	—
Other	—	—	—	—	—	—
Total number of serious obstacles in country	5	5	3	3	0	8

— Not available.
Source: IFC (1999).

The Potential for Private Sector Development

Clearly the provision of an enabling environment for the private sector is key to making the Tanzanian economy competitive. Implementing across-the-board institutional reforms to further improve the administrative and regulatory framework should go a long way toward attracting higher levels of domestic and foreign investment. That said, the country has made substantive progress in introducing broadly based macroeconomic reforms and is pursuing an ambitious structural reform agenda. In view of Tanzania's having successfully completed a series of reforms conducive to fostering private sector development, it would be useful here to identify a select number of "entry points" or areas of competitive advantage where invested resources can earn meaningful returns, and in turn contribute to Tanzania's socioeconomic growth. The areas where Tanzanian private sector potential can be viably unleashed over the next few years thus include, but are by no means limited to, the following:

- *Agriculture, including agribusiness.* This, by sheer force of size and presence in the country, is a clear choice as an area of private sector activity with potential.
- Mining and tourism. In Tanzania, these sectors have a demonstrated advantage and have already had a head start.
- *Infrastructure.* This area has considerable room for greater private sector participation as a large number of publicly held utility and infrastructure entities are placed on the block for sale or lease by the government.

- *Private users.* These have indicated their willingness to pay for quality education beyond the primary level, and for (largely urban) health services, with a commensurate supply response from the private sector.
- *New trends in business.* These represent an emerging area of opportunity that Tanzania should enthusiastically seize. Revolutionary changes have occurred in the way the world does business. These changes are being introduced at a rapid pace by developments in information and communication technologies that could help Tanzania take a giant leap toward meeting its growth and development objectives.

Cost of Doing Business: Tax Policy

As the private sector and the range of economic activities expand, the tax administration responsibilities of the government will increase. The revamped judicial system must provide for an effective commercial court and expeditious tax appeal systems. The government's capacity to assess the specific nature of each industrial segment with respect to prospects, nature of investment, gestation period, debt financing, and the effect of these on generation of real profit and the resultant tax revenue effort must be strengthened. The government must guard against resorting to compensating for its incapacity to collect revenue through ad hoc taxation.

As stated above, to encourage a more robust response of private investment in Tanzania, the government must broadly distribute the incentives across sectors, in contrast to the recent concentration in the enclave sectors of mining and tourism. More than 95 percent of Tanzania's agriculture is privately managed, and this sector accounts for about a half of GDP and contributes up to 70 percent of foreign exchange earnings directly or indirectly (through agro-industry). Therefore, a significant part of the effort in enhancing private sector growth has to target this sector. Reduction in tax and nontax controls and in the opaqueness of agricultural taxation (which raise the costs of business operations) will encourage greater participation by agribusiness and increase the productivity of investment in agriculture. Spreading income-earning opportunities to reach the poor entails encouraging investment in smallholder agriculture as well as in small and medium enterprises in rural areas. It is therefore necessary to pay attention to the poverty-reducing measures of creating high-quality employment opportunities, developing skills, regionally locating enterprises, providing market access, and removing artificial shortages.

Promoting Private Investment in Agriculture across Large and Small Producers and Marketing Agents

Agriculture hosts the largest share of private sector activities in the economy, spanning individual smallholder farmers and large farmers. However, little attention has been paid to what is needed for a robust private sector involvement in it. To a large extent, the basic constraints faced by both categories of farmers are similar in nature. The main differences are related to the commercial operations, which they face in addition to employment issues, and these are international trade-related and taxation bottlenecks. Efforts to improve the private sector environment for investment, commercial production, and processing in the agriculture sector are still nascent and measures are needed toward strengthening a more open and fair trade environment to reduce the cost of doing business.

Broadening Returns from an Enclave Industry: Mining

Given its rich deposits of precious minerals (gold, diamonds, tanzanite, and rubies), industrial minerals (tin, nickel, copper, iron, phosphate, gypsum, graphite, salt, and limestone), and fuels (coal and natural gas), along with the government's liberalization policies in the sector, Tanzania saw an upsurge in international interest in mining exploration in the 1990s. More money was spent in Tanzania on nonferrous minerals exploration in 1998 than in any other African country. The first commercial gold mine started operations in November 1999, with bright prospects of several more projects coming on-stream.

Notwithstanding the high level of investment since 1996, the mining sector's performance has been constrained by inadequate capacity, poor technology, and a lack of capital on the one hand, and high costs of production on the other. These constraints aside, the prospects of Tanzania's mining sector appear promising in the medium term. The incentives the government gives to the sector, which allow, among other things, the repatriation of profits and imports of equipment that are free of duties or value added taxes, have created a most favorable operating environment that is competitive by international standards. In fact, the considerable incentives granted to mining companies, which have not been replicated in other sectors, have prompted some debate within Tanzania as to how the country can benefit more from this industry. Local governments are also seeking to benefit more significantly from mining activity in their regions. The central government currently takes royalties of 3 percent once production comes on line, plus a 35 percent corporation tax (after a 100 percent capital write-off allowance).

However, opening up new mines will only lead to sustained and broader dissemination of benefits in the long term if the Tanzanian Mineral Sector Policy is now finalized. It will ensure prudent management of mineral resources and greater overall transparency and enhanced clarity with respect to health and safety issues. Poor management of the revenues flowing from the sector; corruption; and negative environmental and social consequences that could negate the envisaged benefits of larger mineral exports, increased employment, and higher tax revenues must all be guarded against. In tandem, relevant public institutions, for example, the Ministry of Energy and Minerals, must be strengthened to promote, administer, and regulate private investment in the industrial mining ventures; establish and maintain investor confidence through consistent and transparent legislation for competitive participation in mining; and formulate appropriate rules in mineral rights registration, mine safety, environmental regulations, and monitoring and revenue collection.

Another critical element of the strategy in the outcomes of this enclave sector entails developing and executing a policy and infrastructural framework to promote an effective and sustainable small-scale mining industry. This framework would allow broader sharing. Measures to promote organized artisanal mining and to strengthen partnerships and linkages with large investors (to facilitate technology transfer and optimization of mineral resource exploration) and mineral dealers will encourage formal mineral marketing. This in turn would serve to curb mineral smuggling.

Developing World-Class Tourism

Of Tanzania's total landmass, 15 percent is reserved for tourism, an industry that holds promise for the country's economic future. Neglected and constrained by poor infrastructure over decades, Tanzania is now becoming increasingly popular as a tourist location on the continent. The *Financial Times* (March 31, 1999) special on Tanzania unequivocally notes that,

> From the spectacular game reserves of the Serengeti Park and Ngorongoro crater to the peaks of Kilimanjaro and the crumbling island charm of Zanzibar, Tanzania's tourism industry does not need to lie when it claims to offers one of the world's most complete holiday destinations.

Tanzania's political stability and absence of internal strife and violence, the wide choice of beach and game parks, and the relatively uncrowded destinations have all helped enhance the attractiveness of Tanzania.

The significant increases in tourism revenues and tourist presence are attributed to strengthened publicity and promotion of Tanzanian tourist facilities, including, increased participation by private sector operators and Tanzania Tourist Board staff in various international tourism and trade promotion fairs and improved efforts undertaken by the government in collaboration with donors both to improve tourism services and to enhance technical capacity in the sector. The government aims to sustain visitor levels at around 0.5 million. It also is focusing on diversifying the product and developing newer products, such as cultural tourism. In broad terms, the government's future strategy for the sector is geared toward promoting low-volume, high-yield tourism. A related objective is to improve tourism infrastructure and facilities, particularly in the southern game reserves of Selous and Ruaha (the Southern Circuit), so that the current level of 7.6 days spent in-country by each tourist increases substantively. The government is also aware of the importance of environmental protection as being key to the long-term future of the sector, in addition to peace and security.

Tanzanian tourism clearly stands to benefit from being offered as part of an East African package combining beaches and animals. The Tanzanian tourist industry depends closely on that sector in Kenya, with 66 percent of the tourists arriving by road from Kenya to the northern wildlife area (the Northern Circuit). While earlier efforts to create an East African identity for tourism have not met with success amid bureaucratic disagreements and differences in philosophy, the private sector has confirmed that combinations of Kenyan and Tanzanian itineraries are performing well. However, unless the East African Cooperation's strategic action plan for tourism coordination is adequately implemented, Tanzania is unlikely to reap the full rewards; and glitches, such as the closed borders between the Masai Mara and Serengeti, will continue to impinge on the sector's monetary returns.

The government and the private sector are now recognizing the tourism sector's enormous potential for contributing further to GDP, creating further employment opportunities, boosting foreign exchange receipts, and driving the development of ancillary services. With its abundance of unique, exotic destinations, Tanzania should move ahead to develop its tourism industry in a culturally sensitive and environmentally sustainable way. The government must follow through on the coordinated development and maintenance of the transportation, telecommunication, and banking infrastructure and water supply, at the very least near the Northern Circuit and the coastal region around Zanzibar and Dar es Salaam. Over the long run, the government must not only encourage private investment in the sector, but also effectively coordinate and regulate the sector. In addition, private enterprises must focus on improving the level, reliability, and quality of services to bring Tanzania to the rank of world-class destinations. As noted in the *Financial Times* article, if the Southern Circuit, which boasts the continent's largest game reserve and unparalleled viewing, is revived, Tanzanian tourism can look forward to a prosperous future.

Supporting the Informal Sector

The dynamism of the informal sector in Tanzania needs to be harnessed, given that it is probably the most dynamic and most important source of livelihood for the urban-dwelling poor. Estimates from the last survey of the sector has put its contribution to employment at 22 percent and to GDP at 32 percent. The urban informal sector has been most noteworthy in grassroots efforts to cushion against declines in real incomes, even for those employed in the formal sector at the lower end of the pay scale. It is considered to be the most dynamic in terms of employment generation and productivity growth. It has also thrived in spite of government restrictions and serves as an incubator for emerging local entrepreneurship.

Dynamism and enthusiasm in this sector can be encouraged by removing impediments to its growth and providing a framework for availing credit and supportive infrastructure to small-scale enterprises and trading activities. As stated before, the government need not necessarily constrain this sector's activities, since its contributions are captured by indirect taxes. By taking steps to enhance capacity of the informal sector, NGOs need to further induce improvement in its organization and business orientation.

Past forms of support for the growth of this sector focused on instituting special credit schemes, providing marketing and technological information in support of growth in sales and enhanced productivity, setting up cooperative schemes to foster collaboration in activity, sharing information and enabling realization of scale economies, and providing infrastructure by building industrial estates for small-scale industrial activities. The Small Industries Development Organization has been the main institutional channel for government support to this sector. Most of these efforts by public institutions have been supplemented by nongovernmental agencies. These are initiatives that need to be enlarged for the benefit of wider coverage of participants in this sector.

Technical extension services for small businesses now need to be instituted or expanded to enhance their productivity and managerial efficiency. Links with large producers should be sought and supported through subcontracting, again learning from experiences of economies such as Taiwan (China). Also important in this regard are programs for upgrading skills and production processes, as well as research support for developing new technologies and adapting technologies developed elsewhere for local conditions.

Strengthening Private Provision of Social Services

The challenge of meeting the requirements for providing adequate quantity and quality of social services in Tanzania is immense, more so if the government has to do it alone with only donor support. Private sector participation and contributions by users to financing the costs of providing these requirements are necessary. The interest of the private sector in supplying education services at the postprimary level has been demonstrated. For example, this sector runs nearly half of the secondary schools in the country. Much less involvement has been recorded in primary education, which remains the dominant purview of the public sector. Similarly, private dispensaries and hospitals have recently mushroomed in urban centers, while public services still dominate in rural districts and villages. A natural divide is therefore emerging that can be exploited to concentrate and rationalize the involvement of the public and the private sector in the provision of social services. There is also increasing evidence of the willingness of users to contribute toward financing the costs of these services, provided they are of acceptable quality. The examples here include the introduction of the drug revolving fund, parental contributions in education, and user fees in hospitals. The scope for budgetary relief of providing social services is therefore quite wide. The government should seize this opportunity by eliminating entry barriers to private sector participation while ensuring adherence to the required standards and safety measures.

Improving Infrastructure

The divestiture programs and community-based initiatives now under implementation or preparation in supplying utilities and infrastructure services augur well for greater efficiency in their provision. In particular, water, power, telecommunication, and road services should benefit from private sector inputs. A decisive and well-managed approach to these programs would go a long way toward a cost-effective expansion of these services to the public in support of growth and their well-being. The government's strategy for improving efficiency in infrastructure (utilities) provision is to introduce competition through various forms of private participation in infrastructure, including the privatization of the incumbent utilities. Key elements of effective private participation in infrastructure include privatization of the incumbent utilities, clear rules in bidding procedures for public procurement, and an appropriate regulatory regime. Such participation in infrastructure is widely viewed as a key entry point in that it is seen to support beneficial cumulative spirals in the real economy: more reliable, efficient services; the easing of fiscal constraints on the government; and increased private sector activity. It is also seen to benefit institutional development by placing emphasis on regulatory or judicial aspects, which leads to strengthened national capacity and awareness, and by facilitating transfer of technology and management skills (World Bank 1998). It is important in this regard to ensure that private participation in infrastructure fits well within the overall sectoral reform and development strategy of Tanzania and contributes toward the investment and performance goals of the country.

To provide an effective enabling environment for attracting increased private participation in these key sectors in the medium to long run, Tanzania is now focusing on the creation of new sectoral regulatory laws and independent cross-sectoral regulatory institutions to progressively build the needed modern economic regulatory capacity. Establishing effective infrastructure regulatory capacity and preparing and implementing Tanzania's privatization program in key infrastructure, banking and insurance, and agriculture are critical both to the development of a robust private sector and to the enhanced economic growth of the country. Regulatory reforms will be sequenced to create procompetitive regulatory environments before the divestiture of public enterprises in the sectors concerned through the creation of clear, transparent regulatory rules built into concession contracts and the buildup of regulatory capacity.

The regulatory frameworks for industries such as telecommunications, energy, water, ports, and railways will play a critical role in successful privatization. To minimize the need for regulatory intervention, reform should be focused on encouraging competition wherever possible. Where regulation is required to provide the necessary investor confidence, most of the rules regulating price and service conditions must ensure that there is little room for regulatory discretion and must be embodied in contracts backed up by international arbitration. Effective regulatory institutions will be required in this environment to monitor and enforce these rules. In the long term, when investor confidence has been established in the institutions, sectoral rules can then be developed that provide more flexibility for adjusting to changing economic circumstances and that provide stronger incentives for efficiency. The government intends to focus on developing sector-specific frameworks sufficient for privatization to proceed and on establishing the basic institutional arrangements. It is essential that there is full consolidation and harmonization within and between sectoral frameworks and institutions.

A recent starting point for the rehabilitation of road networks has been the main arteries connecting the countryside and the main consuming centers and export points. Upgrade of these strategic links is essential for ensuring the basic minimum connectivity needed to move produce over long distances, which will reduce marketing costs and improve accessibility.

Long periods of neglect in maintenance and curtailment of development budgets for achieving fiscal balance has led to a serious deterioration of transport networks. Poor mobility, in turn, has hampered efficiency in production, supply responsiveness, and market integration. As the road improvement program gathers momentum, the need for clear commitments in the budgetary provision for recurrent maintenance costs should be emphasized. Such earmarking approaches have been developed through targeting revenue from user charges for maintenance of the infrastructure. The establishment and protection of the Road Fund in 1998 was a step in this direction. The process of establishing an independent road agency is in progress. Most critical in this regard is strengthening the management capability of the government to prioritize investment and develop an effective maintenance system that pays greater attention to cost-effectiveness. Where traffic demand permits, a system in which the government builds, operates, and then transfers ownership of road networks to the private sector could be contemplated.

The next phase ought to be the development of feeder roads into and from these arteries to reach the production points in rural areas. A clear strategy under the next Integrated Roads Program needs to be developed to focus on a cost-effective and sustainable feeder-road program. Such a strategy should also explore the possibility of engaging local contractors to make effective use of the trained capacity from the initiative described above as well as schemes such as "food for work," which have proved successful in several countries where they have been tried. Cost considerations are important, but such schemes, where they are feasible, pay a double dividend by providing opportunities for the poor to raise their consumption while at the same time improving road networks. Given that such schemes have often used rural labor in the agricultural off-season, they have helped to expand opportunities for rural employment to supplement the dominant agricultural activities.

An important area of infrastructure is communication. The value of information flow in raising productivity and improving education and health status cannot be overstated. The critical consideration here is availing affordable means of communications. Until recently the government had total monopoly of the communication systems. Legislation has now been amended to permit private providers. The response has been tremendous, with rapid mushrooming of daily papers, radio stations, and television stations and cost-reducing competition in telephony. These changes have broadened the scope of information and the means of conveying it availed to the broad range of citizens. Improvements in education can now be better exploited for innovation and social interaction. Effectiveness of education and agricultural extension services can also be improved through providing more information through better communication means. This trend should be encouraged, and providers of education services, extension services, and health education should make better use of improved means for the flow of information.

Improved access to a low-cost and stable power supply is a significant catalyst for private sector investment and efficient business operations. The focus in the past two decades has been on expanding the supply of power and developing the national grid system for arterial distribution countrywide. With the commissioning of the Kihansi and Songo Songo hydroelectric projects, the power supply capacity will increase significantly. A key issue is a cost-effective distribution system. Preparations for the privatization of the distribution system are now ongoing and will lead to substantial cost reduction, which, if passed through to users, will significantly reduce business cost.

The distribution of power through rural electrification and other forms of energy has lagged behind other developments in the power sector and now needs greater attention. The majority of the rural population, and for that matter of low-income urban dwellers, depends on forest resources for energy. Rural electrification and promotion of using fossil fuel is thus important—not only for improving the quality of life and for providing needed energy sources for production but, more important, for preserving the quality of land. Environmental protection initiatives will gain considerably from the development and distribution of energy sources other than fuel wood.

While communication technologies are becoming increasingly pervasive, Tanzanian businesses have yet to exploit this opportunity in a significant way. Indeed, in general the technology used by a broad swathe of private sector entities, especially by small and medium enterprises, is outmoded. This creates issues of quality and standards, especially in regard to external markets. Constraints to adopting modern technology range from the high cost of acquisition to the low profit margins that do not justify additional technology-related costs. Equally important is the low skill base of the general work force, which makes technology adoption and use even more complex. While the use of the Internet and other information communication technologies is skewed toward the better-off segments within the better-off economies, the World Wide Web is an instrument that, if made widely available and accessible, can in the long run help reduce knowledge and economic inequities.

Still, the revolution in information communication technologies is slowly but steadily taking root across the country. At present, five Internet service providers are based in Dar es Salaam, serving a variety of clients. The services of these providers encompass distribution, publishing, provision of Internet media platforms, as well as a broad range of e-commerce businesses related to support functions. In addition, protocols for public-key (cryptography) infrastructure are being refined and expanded. The government is joining in as well: the Parastatal Reform Commission, the Government of Tanzania's privatization agency, recently launched its own Web site. The site provides, for example, updates on divestitures currently under way and information on the privatization process in Tanzania, on companies to be privatized, on labor standards, on environmental regulations, and on implementation of Uruguay Round Agreements. Various other public agencies and ministries (for example, the Tanzania Tourism Board and the Ministry of Energy and Minerals) have their own Web sites.

However, Tanzania now stands at a crossroads, where taking the wrong direction will have incalculable costs for the country that amount to fairly comprehensive economic isolation. By the same token, going (even if somewhat belatedly) the way the rest of the world is headed could lead to massive economic growth and resultant poverty alleviation for Tanzania. The high-speed developments in online business technology—defying geographic boundaries and time constraints—are transforming the economic face of the world. This transformation is no less critical than the industrial revolution of the 1900s and must be taken seriously. As various classified ads proclaim with one voice, "it is either e-business or out of business." For Tanzania, bridging the information gap through appropriate information communication technologies can contribute to accelerated growth and to increased industrial productivity and agricultural potential, in due course, from enhanced efficacy of the private (and public) sectors. Civil society empowerment and the promulgation of an effective democratic system of government; improved quality of life; and enriched development of media, culture, and community are some of the other contributions of the Internet revolution that is pervading every facet of the global society and economy today.

English-speaking nations with relatively low labor costs and high skills, such as India and the Philippines, are cashing in on the global dispersion of business, acting as magnets attracting international jobs and substantial revenues. The government must move rapidly to promote sound primary and secondary education to build an educated and skilled labor force. (The state of Tamil Nadu, India, alone spends US$10 million a year on computer literacy in local schools.) This must be buttressed by boosting investments in infrastructure, especially power and telecommunication networks. Again in India, the government has facilitated rapid information and communication technology (ICT) sector development by endorsing information technology parks and software technology parks and recently agreed to increased Internet bandwidth, providing global-class infrastructure. Eliminating red tape, instituting an encouraging, state-of-the-art policy agenda, including a transparent, cohesive tax regime for ICT industry will be conducive to its growth, as will government action to develop a well-thought through and integrated ICT strategic framework. The government needs to be at the vanguard of these developments and the passage of an information technology bill and cyber laws by Parliament should facilitate further growth of software and e-commerce industries.

Figure 6.1. *Tanzania: Incentives, Politics/Institutions, Sources of Growth, PSD Tools, and Outcomes*

Incentives and politics/institutions	Sources of growth	PSD tools	Outcomes
ANALYSIS	SECTORS	ACTIONS	LEARNING

Macro (fiscal, monetary, exchange)
- Adjustment

Public
- Reformers and laggards

Endowments
- Natural, human and infrastructural

Microeconomic
- Trade and market liberalization (services, labor, finance)

Private
- Industrial structure (small and medium enterprises, public enterprises, etc.)
- Institutional structure (chambers of commerce, trade associations)

- Agriculture and agribusiness
- Mining
- Tourism
- Private participation in infrastructure
- Social services
- E-commerce

- Roll-back government
- Strengthen financial, legal, judicial and regulatory underpinnings
- Transform domestic perceptions
- Mitigate risks
- Develop sound infrastructure
- Attract foreign investment
- Strengthen regional linkages
- Develop robust export performance
- Nurture small and medium enterprises
- Foster enterprise learning

- Develop broad-based growth
- Implement feedback, monitoring and evaluation systems
- Strengthen strategic underpinnings

Source: Adapted from World Bank (1998).

74

7. PACEMAKERS FOR SUSTAINABLE GROWTH

The key to significant poverty reduction in Tanzania is accelerated growth. Policy-based projections that take into account recent improvements in the policy and institutional framework indicate that per capita GDP could grow between 1.4 and 1.9 percent annually. Further improvements in this framework would raise the predicted annual rate of growth of per capita GDP to an estimated range of 2.4–4.3 percent. Estimates of poverty elasticities indicate that such accelerated growth could lead to a reduction in the share of the population living below the poverty line, from around 50 percent currently to 30 percent by 2015 (see table 7.1).

Table 7.1. *Policy-Based Growth Projections, GDP Per Capita*
(*percent*)

	1999 rating	*Constant policy*	*Improve +0.5*	*Improve +1.0*
Country Policy and Institutional Assessments (World Bank)	3.55	1.80	2.88	3.95
Euromoney	2.22	1.67	2.31	2.95
International Country Rating Group	3.38	1.39	1.90	2.41
Institutional	1.97	1.85	3.07	4.30
Average	2.77	1.68	2.54	3.40

Sources: World Bank and other sources as indicated.

Sustaining peace and tranquility, stability, and national cohesiveness is critical for development. Tanzania has managed to forge national cohesiveness and enjoyed peace and stability throughout the postindependence period, except for the six-month war with Uganda under Idi Amin. For Tanzania to realize its growth potential, it must nurture and sustain the current peaceful atmosphere, both within the country and also with its neighbors.

Governance matters for long-term growth not only because of its effects on policy distortions and uncertainty, but also because of its capacity to handle external shocks. Going by the observation that the neopatrimonial governance was not progrowth, Tanzania is now posed to exploit the benefits of the open political regime it adopted in 1995.

The HIV/AIDS pandemic seriously threatens Tanzania's socioeconomic development. The epidemic has already had a huge effect on overall human development. The relative high incidence of HIV/AIDS has led to a drastic decline in some indicators related to human development and eliminated gains in life expectancy that had been painstakingly achieved during the past four decades. Recent studies of the impact of HIV/AIDS on economic growth indicate that at present incidence levels, economic growth will be 1 percent lower than without HIV/AIDS. Taking measures to halt the spread of HIV/AIDS thus has to be central to Tanzania's development efforts.

Achieving the target of accelerated growth will require significant efforts to enhance productivity and increase investment in both human and physical capital. The removal of institutional and policy constraints under the ongoing reforms is an important element in closing the productivity gap that has opened up over the past 20 years. As this gap closes, higher rates of growth can be generated from more efficient use of existing capacities. However, further increases in productivity will only be possible if close attention is paid to the acquisition, adoption, and use of various forms of knowledge, including technical know-how. FDI, an appropriate communication and information infrastructure, and improvements in the level of educational attainment are key to facilitating productivity gains through knowledge.

Increasing the investment in human capital requires implementing measures that will not only increase the incentives for and returns to undertaking such investments, but also requires increased public support in areas where externalities are large, such as primary education and preventive health care. Increased public resource allocations to these areas have to be accompanied by increases in the efficiency of service delivery if the desired increase in the stock of human capital is to be achieved. Particular attention needs to be paid to the quality of education and its relevance to the demands of the labor market. Given the rapidly changing demands of the labor market, emphasis needs to be placed on the acquisition of strong skills in numeracy and literacy and on the ability to acquire new knowledge through lifelong learning.

Investment in physical capital is the final element necessary for sustaining high growth rates. One of the key lessons of Tanzania's postindependence experience is the importance of a clear separation of areas of public and private investment. The principal source of investment has to be the private sector. However, public investment has an important role to play in providing selected infrastructure services that are complementary to private investments and that are unlikely to be provided by the private sector in sufficient quantities. Another important role for government in this area is providing an appropriate legal and regulatory framework for private sector investment and ensuring property rights and legal contracts. Thus, one of the imperatives for the immediate future is to continue reforms to improve the environment for private sector investment. An area of equal importance is the development of financial markets. At present, financial intermediation is barely working. This constrains both the savings rate and the flow of savings to the most productive uses. In addition to domestic savings from both the private and public sector, foreign savings can also be an important source of finance for domestic investment. While significant resource transfers currently take place in the form of ODA, these will need to be supplemented by increased inflows of private capital to finance increased investment levels in the private sector.

The realization of a higher investment level will require bold and pragmatic policy actions to increase the savings effort. First is curtailing unproductive expenditure, fraud, and waste, which would provide a significant potential for increasing public sector savings. These increased savings could then finance public investments and keep the government from having to access Tanzania's domestic credit market. Second is encouraging private savings through contractual savings institutions by pushing through the just started liberalization of the insurance market. Added to this would be the implementation of a comprehensive pension reform, including liberalization of the pension system. The other potential source of increased savings is the introduction of tax-driven savings instruments, such as five-year, tax-free deposits. In addition, the country must accelerate and sustain the reform of its financial sector and institutions, consolidate the stability of macroeconomic fundamentals, and encourage remittances from abroad by judiciously removing the remaining capital controls.

Foreign aid can play an important role in supporting economic and social development. Tanzania is one of the biggest aid recipients on a per capita basis. In the past, the effective use of foreign aid was hampered by a poor policy environment, inadequate attention to the institutional capacity for effective and efficient delivery of public services, and limited state capacity for the effective management of foreign aid. Policy reforms undertaken during the past decade set the stage for a higher development impact of foreign aid in Tanzania. In addition, attention also needs be paid to specific issues concerning the use of foreign aid. Key among these is a better integration of foreign aid flows into the government budget to ensure that the recurrent cost implications of donor financed investment are properly taken into account. Closely linked to this is the gradual move from project aid to general budget support. This requires further improvements in budget management, accountability and transparency to provide donors sufficient assurance that their funds are being properly used. In addition, it also requires the strengthening of public sector capacities and efficiency for effective public service delivery. Apart from capacity-building initiatives, these efforts also need to address the low motivation of the civil service and its ability to attract and retain high caliber personnel.

Structural transformation—that is, an increase in the share of value added by industry and services, with a matching relative decline in the importance of agriculture—can be expected to occur alongside accelerated growth. Although the secondary and tertiary sector will grow in all likelihood at significant higher rates than agriculture, this implies by no means that this growth should come at the expense of agriculture. Rather, the opposite is true. Agriculture will, for the foreseeable future, remain the backbone of the economy, and only a prospering agriculture sector can provide the basis for sustainable poverty reduction and accelerated growth in the other sectors. A potential expansion of manufacturing activities in Tanzania will have to take advantage of various factors specific to the country. These include:

- Easy access to international trade through Tanzania's three sea ports, whose efficiency is being improved through privatization measures.
- A significantly increased and effective power supply from hydro and thermal sources.
- Significant, though not yet fully developed, iron, coal, mineral, and gas deposits.
- A stable macroeconomic and political environment.

The main constraints in the medium to long term are likely to be the low level of skills and educational attainment among Tanzania's population and an only rudimentary system of financial intermediation. As progress in these two areas is extremely time consuming, it is imperative that serious efforts to achieve improvements in these areas remain high on the policy agenda and are vigorously pursued (see table 7.2).

Table 7.2. *Scenarios for Economic Growth and Structural Transformation*
(*percent*)

Sector	Actual share in GDP, 1998	Slow growth		Medium growth		Fast growth	
		Average real growth rate, 1998–2005	Share in GDP, 2025	Average real growth rate, 1998–2005	Share in GDP, 2025	Average real growth rate, 1998–2005	Share in GDP, 2025
Agriculture	46	3.2	40	3.2	30	3.2	20
Industry	14	4.8	18	6.5	20	10.0	30
Services	40	4.0	42	5.9	50	7.7	50
Total	100	3.8	100	5.0	100	6.7	100

Source: World Bank staff estimates.

Tanzania's rich resource endowment offers the opportunity to garner additional growth from more intensive exploitation of its resource base. Exports of agricultural commodities, increased activity in the mining sector, and expansion of tourism are three areas that already have registered relatively high growth rates in recent years, but which still have substantial potential for additional growth in the near future. However, because some of these activities are enclaves within the economy, they have only weak linkages to the rest of the economy, limiting their potential to contribute in a significant way to poverty reduction. It is thus imperative to take measures that increase the linkages with the rest of the economy, such as creating incentives for the reinvestment of proceeds from these sectors in other parts of the Tanzanian economy. Experience from other resource-rich countries demonstrates that, if not carefully managed, natural resource exploitation can have negative effects on economic growth through reduced incentives for private investment in education and other sectors of the economy. In addition, increased public revenue from the taxation of these resources may give rise to political pressures that lead to poor public spending choices. To mitigate these potentially negative effects of increased income from natural resource exploitation, a proper regulatory framework, a strong public finance management system, measures to offset the negative effects on private spending on education, and attention to real exchange rate developments are necessary.

Given the small size of the Tanzanian economy, growth will only be sustainable if it is firmly rooted in international competitiveness and the aggressive pursuit of export opportunities. While the strategic pursuit of opportunities for preferential access to markets is also important, these opportunities are bound to become less so with the phasing in of the new World Trade Organization rules and regulations, putting an even greater premium on measures that enhance international competitiveness. The deepening of regional integration within existing arrangements such as the East African Cooperation and the Southern Africa Development Community also plays an important role in this area. While the enlarging of markets is an important aspect of regional integration, equally important benefits are likely to arise from positive neighborhood effects, such as policy and growth spillovers, network externalities from infrastructure, or increased attractiveness of the region as a manufacturing location for multinational corporations.

8. TOWARD A MEDIUM-TERM PROGRAM OF ACTION FOR TANZANIA'S DEVELOPMENT

In looking forward, this memorandum concludes by suggesting elements of a desirable program of action for Tanzania's development strategy in the medium term. It takes as a point of its departure, Tanzania's intention to build on the strengths of peace, unity, and self esteem and to break with the past weaknesses in economic management.

National Vision 2025

This intention is amply exposed in *The Tanzania Vision 2025* (URT 1998b), and the reform programs pursued for nearly a decade and a half, albeit with some punctuation in the first half of the 1990s. Vision 2025 is used in the report both as a statement of hope and to provide a reference point to determine what is feasible and desirable.

The Tanzania National Development Vision 2025 has three main objectives: achieving a high-quality livelihood for Tanzanians, attaining good governance through the rule of law, and developing a strong and competitive economy. A high-quality livelihood includes improvements in access to basic consumption needs, increased longevity and quality of life (better education and health and safe water), improved survival rates for the young, and gender equality in all these respects. Good governance and rule of law encompass absence of corruption, a society with self-confidence and security, and strong respect for the rule of law. A strong and competitive economy is characterized as a diversified and semi-industrialized economy with sustained macroeconomic stability, growing at 8 percent annually, with an efficient infrastructure and capable of being a competitive player in the increasingly integrating global economy.

A Medium-Term Strategy toward Achieving the Development Vision

A medium-term strategy for achieving long-term targets of Tanzania's National Development Vision 2025 necessarily centers on sustainable reduction of the poverty that afflicts half of its population. From the foregoing, such a strategy should rest on four pillars: a growth strategy that reduces poverty, a public service delivery system that is of higher quality and more cost-effective, containment of the spread and management of the impacts of the HIV/AIDS pandemic, and a governance structure that promotes accountability and social inclusion and upholds basic rights to a decent livelihood. In keeping with the comprehensive development approach, the key elements of Tanzania's development strategy, while focused on one major goal, identifies a set of complementary interventions most potent for success. It builds on past and ongoing successful actions and learns from the weaknesses of past efforts. Table 8.1 presents the main elements of the strategy, delineating the main strategic interventions needed for sustained reduction of poverty, ongoing reforms or actions, and areas for further action to achieve the goals of the strategy.

Table 8.1. *Toward a Medium-Term Plan of Action for Tanzania's Development*

Long-term goals (Vision 2025 and NPES)	Strategies	Actions	Instruments/ Programs
Strong and competitive economy			
▪ Growth rate 8% per year or more ▪ Diversified and semi-industrialized economy	▪ Scaling up growth and diversifying the economy - Create an environment conducive for economic expansion of 6%–7% per year	▪ Consolidate and sustain macroeconomic stability ▪ Continue policy and institutional reforms for market friendly environment ▪ Reduce the cost of doing business and create capital-friendly environment for private sector ▪ Exploit new opportunities (agriculture, manufacturing, mining, and tourism) for rapid growth and modernization of the economy	PRGF PSAC TAS PRSP
High-quality livelihood			

▪ No racial and gender imbalances
▪ No abject income poverty
▪ Well educated society
▪ Access to primary health care for all
▪ Reduced infant and maternal mortality, by 75%.
	▪ Building a cost effective and better quality system of public service delivery
	  - Improve strategic prioritization of expenditure
	  - Adopt result-orientation as the main monitoring approach for effectiveness of public spending (value for money)
	  - Strengthen competencies and institutional capacity for managing public service programs
	▪ Promoting longevity of life (survival) through better health and combating HIV/AIDS pandemic
	  - Contain the spread of HIV/AIDS infection
	  - Manage the impact of HIV/AIDS
		▪ Mainstream the strategic priority expenditure allocation and determine public investment programs under MTEF
		▪ Widen stakeholder consultation and ensure full integration of external finance into MTEF for effective application of resources and high impact on poverty reduction
		▪ Design sector development programs to optimize cross-sector synergies
		▪ Determine outputs (through PER process) expected from application of allocated funds
		▪ Undertake value-for-money audits and reviews
		▪ Bring the audits and reviews into public domain through the PER process
		▪ Use performance budgeting and performance improvement modules under PSRP to entrench the culture of result orientation
		▪ Build personnel and institutional capacity
		▪ Institute pay reform (motivation)
		▪ Rationalize the functions of governments to purely public activities
		▪ Contract out activities requiring commercially available specialized skills
		▪ Adopt national HIV/AIDS policy and strengthen the National AIDS Control Committee to lead nationwide, multisectoral efforts against HIV/AIDS
		▪ Make available through the budget, as guided by MTEF, financial resources for containing the spread and managing impacts of HIV/AIDS
		▪ Strengthen the capacity of NACP (research, surveillance, dissemination of HIV/AIDS reports)
		▪ Intensify anti-HIV/AIDS campaigns countrywide
		▪ Introduce HIV/AIDS, public health, and peer education in schools
		▪ Involve local communities, political leaders, nongovernmental organizations, religious groups, and donors in mass education and campaigns against HIV/AIDS
		▪ Ensure availability of affordable treatment of the already infected people
		▪ Involve and offer support to local communities, nongovernmental organizations, and religious groups in providing safety nets to HIV/AIDS victims—orphans and the very elderly
			PER
			MTEF
			TAS
			PER
			CAG reports
			PRSP
			PSRP
			LGRP
			PRSP
			NACP
			PER

Good governance and rule of law			

▪ Accountability
▪ No corruption
▪ Peace and stability
▪ Reward for good performance
	▪ Building more transparent, accountable and tolerant governance system
	  - Promote social inclusion
	  - Strengthen accountability
	  - Deal with corruption
		▪ Enable participation in the development process by all citizens
		▪ Devolve responsibilities for managing development to local authorities
		▪ Bring accountability systems into the public domain
		▪ Sustain freedom of media and improve flow of information through effective means of communication
		▪ Deal with grand corruption so as to reduce the cost of doing business and to encourage investment
		▪ Scale up attention to petty corruption in judiciary, police, taxation, education, and health at the local level
			LGRP
			PER
			NACS

Acronyms: CAG (Controller and Auditor General), LGRP (Leading Group for Poverty Reduction), MTEF (Medium-Term Expenditure Framework), NACP (National AIDS Control Programme), NACS (National Anti-Corruption Strategy), NPES (National Poverty Eradication Strategy), PER (Public Expenditure Review), PRGF (Poverty Reduction Growth Facility of the International Monetary Fund), PRSP (Poverty Reduction Strategy Paper), PSAC (Programmatic Structural Adjustment Credit of the World Bank), PSRP (Public Service Reform Program), TAS (Tanzania Assistance Strategy)
Source: Authors.

A poverty-focused growth strategy requires actions in three main areas. First is to create an environment that is conducive to scaling up economic expansion from the current rate of 4–5 percent to 6–7 percent. The main means for achieving this target include:

- Consolidating and sustaining the recent gains in macroeconomic stability.
- Continuing policy and institutional reforms for building a market-friendly environment.
- Reducing the cost of doing private business (especially infrastructure and burdensome taxation) and creating a capital-friendly environment to harness private sector initiative for higher contribution to growth.
- Strategically exploiting new opportunities for rapid growth and modernization of the economy through improved performance of the "traditional" productive sectors (agriculture and manufacturing), sustainable and judicious expansion of some of the newer pacemakers for growth (mining and tourism), and diversification into new opportunities for rapid growth and modernization (for example, nurturing the nascent ICT service sector).

The initial phase of scaling up growth needs to focus on raising productivity, particularly in the dominant sector of agriculture, while benefits from an improved policy environment take root and lead to a higher private investment response in the key sectors mentioned above. Following a successful macroeconomic stabilization, the government has made commitments under the Poverty Reduction and Growth Facility to sustain macroeconomic stability by continuing to contain monetary expansion to noninflationary levels and by upholding fiscal discipline to spur a further reduction of inflation to below 5 percent. Under the Programmatic Structural Adjustment Credit from the International Development Association, the government has also committed to developing a medium-term framework for strengthening the base for a prudent, accountable, and transparent fiscal management; improving the business environment through a more transparent legal system governing commercial operations, safeguarding property rights, and reducing the burden of taxation; more efficiently providing infrastructure services by increasing private sector involvement in transport and utilities; and developing a procompetition regulatory framework. The challenge is to implement the actions in the next four years as envisaged in the framework.

The second area for action is ensuring that benefits from higher growth are shared widely, opportunities for the poor to gainful employment must be expanded. Higher growth of agriculture, a vibrant informal sector and micro-, small-, and medium-size enterprises are particularly pertinent for such broadly based growth. Key to raising agricultural growth is increased productivity. Improved access to markets, particularly through improved rural roads; intensification programs with more timely access to advice and more cost-effective input and credit availability; and removal of disincentives to investment and production make up the main measures for success. The growth of activities under the informal sector and micro-, small-, and medium-size enterprises can benefit mainly from technological extension services and supportive infrastructure such as industrial parks and marketing services. At the same time, to maximize employment impacts, efforts should be made to design labor-intensive approaches for the rehabilitation and maintenance of the rural roads network and to maximize multiplier effects and employment benefits from the growth pacemakers—mining and tourism.

The third area for action is to strengthen human capabilities in support of growth and doing so in a way that increase the capacities of the poor to exploit new opportunities from growth. Previous analysis had identified low levels of education attainment and ill health to be among the major constraints to growth and impacts of improvements in these on growth were assessed to be quite significant. Educating mothers has been shown to have a particularly strong effect on increased demand for education by their future offspring (a valuable intergenerational trait), compounding the positive effects of current support to the sector. This view of social service provision goes beyond the traditional view of education and health as welfare measures, to highlight them as key elements of human capabilities for supporting growth. While for the poor, improved access to basic education and primary health services is of highest priority to help bolster their income earning capabilities, overall economywide improvement in skills and knowledge is needed to cope with competition in the rapidly integrating global economy. The ability to absorb and adapt technology, particularly information technology, is of paramount importance for overall productivity enhancement. The nascent efforts in Tanzania for promoting e-commerce and electronic public service offer opportunities to leapfrog technologically into the 21st century. Essential for exploiting this opportunity is strengthening the coverage of secondary education through higher enrollment rates and better quality teaching, particularly English, which is the information technology lingua franca.

Building Competencies and Strengthening Accountability for Improved Public Service Delivery

The government has in the past five years intensified the process of rationalizing its functions by scaling back its dominant involvement in commercial activities and virtual monopoly in the provision of social services. Through the privatization program and liberalization of markets, the private sector is increasingly making inroads into the previously solely public sector activities, including infrastructure. The participation of the private sector in the provision of social services is also increasing. A strategic division of roles is apparently emerging, with the public sector still being dominant in the provision of basic education and primary health, particularly in the rural areas where poverty is most prevalent. As the government rationalizes its functions, greater attention must also be paid to the cost-effectiveness of providing higher quality public services.

This entails three main areas of action: improving strategic prioritization of expenditure; adopting a results orientation as the main monitoring approach for effectiveness of public spending (value for money); and strengthening competencies and institutional capacity for managing public service programs prudently, particularly at the local government level, where the responsibility for delivery of essential services will increasingly rest. The first area is mainstreaming the strategic priority expenditure allocation approach under an MTEF and making this a central instrument for determining public investment programs. The TAS provides broad guidelines for prioritization and a guide to procedural best practice in external financing relations, but the main operative instrument for integrating aid into the budget system is the MTEF. Wide stakeholder consultation and full integration of external finance into this framework will ensure that programs are demand driven and that resources are applied to those activities with the highest potential impact on poverty reduction. Sector development programs should be designed to maximize on cross-sector synergies to the same end.

The second area for action is moving toward a results orientation and away from the traditional approach of accountability on the inputs side (that is, ascertaining proper use of availed resources). Under the PER process, preliminary work for the definition of production functions of the various sectors is being carried out, which will enable this determination of outputs expected from application of allocated funds. Value-for-money audits and reviews will ground this approach to impact assessment in a new form of accountability. Bringing such reviews increasingly into the public domain through the now inclusive PER process will enhance the effectiveness of accountability systems and develop desired incentives for performance improvement. Performance budgeting and performance improvement modules under the Public Sector Reform Program are important instruments for entrenching the culture of a results orientation.

Finally, the other side of the coin, of course, is to enable public servants and institutions charged with the responsibility for delivery of public services to do so competently and with requisite motivation. Personnel and institutional capacity building and pay reform are therefore essential for strengthening the system for delivering public services. The operation of the Integrated Financial Management System and timely, as well as comprehensive, audits require professional skills and computer literacy. These improvements are complemented by further rationalizing the functions of governments to a more limited range of activities that cannot be more efficiently supplied by the private sector or have considerable externalities to the society. Contracting out activities that require commercially available specialized skills, such as auditing and some aspects of procurement, will also help reduce the use of substandard skills because of the inability to attract and retain such specialized skills in the government. Rationalization reduces pressure on the limited professional capacity of the government. Again the Public Sector Reform Program contains the planned actions in both respects and its successful implementation over the next 10 years is fundamental to increased effectiveness in delivering public services.

Combating the Spread and Managing the Impact of the HIV/AIDS Pandemic

The spread of HIV/AIDS is one of the major threats to economic development in Tanzania. The pandemic is most rampant in the 15–59 age group, which is the productive prime age cohort. The disease, therefore, has a negative impact on production and life expectancy and increases the dependency ratio. In this regard HIV/AIDS has to be viewed, from a wider perspective as a development problem and not purely as a health problem. One measure of reducing poverty has to be the fight against the spread and the impacts of the disease. In combating the spread and impacts of the pandemic, the government has now taken it onboard as one of the priority areas and the current budget has allocated a vote as one of the expenditure items. In this regard, HIV/AIDS prevention and care is a development priority in Tanzania.

A number of actions could be taken to combat the spread and impacts of HIV/AIDS. These actions include:

- Adopting a national policy on HIV/AIDS that cuts across disciplinary and sectoral divides and provides the political and legal framework for an accelerated response.
- Making available financial resources for HIV/AIDS in a planned manner and allocating them through the PER as guided by the MTEF.
- Strengthening the National Aids Control Program in terms of capacity and resources to be able to do research, monitoring, and wide dissemination of timely reports about the status of HIV/AIDS in the country.
- Intensifying the anti-HIV/AIDS campaigns country-wide.
- Introducing HIV/AIDS, public health, and peer education in schools.
- Ensuring an intensive involvement of the local communities, political leaders, NGOs, donors and religious groups in mass education and campaigns against the epidemic, with the objective of reducing the stigma associated with HIV/AIDS by speaking openly about the problem and its reality in their own professional and personal lives.
- Strengthening the National Aids Control Committee, to establish a national body with a clear mandate and the authority to lead a nationwide, multisectoral response to HIV/AIDS and with the institutional capacity and resources to fulfill this mandate.
- Ensuring availability of affordable treatment of the already infected population.

Building a Transparent, Accountable, and Tolerant Governance System

Apart from reducing income poverty, a strategy for poverty reduction has as one of its main objectives improving the social wellbeing of the poor. Longevity of life (survival) can be promoted through better health and combating pandemics such as HIV/AIDS. There are three other aspects to social well-being, influenced mainly by the governance system that is in place, which need attention under a development strategy. They are social inclusion, accountability of public services, and flow of information.

Social inclusiveness is a basis for a meaningful participation in the development process by all concerned citizens. It creates space for expression of priorities in development, and for eliciting unleashing commitment and community initiative in development programs. As Tanzania continues its efforts in building democracy, social inclusion will increasingly become a right. The ongoing devolution of responsibilities for managing development to local governments and community organizations, and bringing accountability systems into the public domain augur well for promoting inclusiveness. Sustaining freedom of media and improving the flow of information through better and more effective means of communication constitute key forms of strategic actions to this end.

In a corrupt environment, the poor are particularly vulnerable to injustice as they cannot afford the means for paying off corrupt officials. Petty corruption in local administration or taxation, and corruption among the judiciary as well the police, are particularly bothersome. Therefore, apart from dealing with grand corruption, which typically raises the cost of doing business and discourages investment, it is imperative that attention be paid to petty corruption in judiciary, police, taxation, and education and health at the local level. The anticorruption strategy will need to scale up attention to this level of corruption.

It can be done, play your part. **What is needed is national resolve to proceed, with increased attention paid to effectiveness in application of resources, and in creating a conducive environment and a space for private initiative.**[5]

---

[5] Taken from an address by President Mwalimu Julius K. Nyerere on the Tanganyika Five-Year Plan and Review of the Plan in May 1964.

REFERENCES

Al-Samarrai, S. Donecker, and B. Reilly. Forthcoming. "Urban and Rural Differences in Primary School Attendance: An Empirical Study for Tanzania." Processed.

Appleton, S., and A. Balihuta. 1996. "Education and Agricultural Productivity in Uganda."*Journal of International Development* 8(3): 415-44.

Appleton, S., and J. Mackinon. 1996. "Enhancing Human Capacities in Africa." In B. Ndulu and N. Van de Walle, eds., *Agenda for Africa's Economic Renewal*. Washington D.C.: Overseas Development Institute.

Bloom, D., and J. Sachs. 1998. *Geography, Demography, and Economic Growth in Africa*. Brookings Papers on Economic Activity. Washington, D.C.

Bol, D. 1995. "Employment and Equity Issues." In L. A. Msambichaka, A. A. L. Kilindo, and G. D. Mjema, eds., *Beyond Structural Adjustment Programmes in Tanzania*. Dar es Salaam: Economic Research Bureau.

Cuddington, J. T. 1993. "Modeling the Macroeconomic Effects of AIDS with an Application to Tanzania." *World Bank Economic Review* 7(2): 173-88.

Delgado, C. L. 1996. "The Role of Smallholder Income Generation from Agriculture in Sub-Saharan Africa." In L. Haddad, ed.,*Achieving Food Security in Southern Africa: New Challenges, New Opportunities*. Washington, D.C.: International Food Policy Research Institute.

Devarajan, S., W. Easterly. and H. Pack. 1999. "Is Investment in Africa Too Low or Too High ?" World Bank, Washington, D.C. Processed.

Eele, G., J. Semboja, S. B. Likwelile, L. Rutasitara, and S. Akroyd. 1999. "Meeting the International Development Targets in Tanzania." Research on Poverty Alleviation and Oxford Policy Management, Dar es Salaam. Draft report.

Filmer, Deon. 1999. *Educational Attainment and Enrollment Profiles: A Resource "Book" based on an Analysis of Demographic and Health Survey Data.*Washington, D.C.: World Bank.

IFPRI (International Food Policy Research Institute) and World Bank. 2000.*Agriculture in Tanzania Since 1986. Follower or Leader of Growth?* Washington, D.C.: IFPRI.

IFC (International Finance Corporation). 1999.*Trends in Private Investment in Development Countries*. Discussion Paper no. 37. Washington, D.C.

Kenny, C., and M. Syrquin. 1999. "Growth and Transformation in East Africa." In S. Yusuf, ed., *Tanzania Peri-urban Development in the African Mirror*, vol. 2. Report no. 1952TA. Washington, D.C.: World Bank.

Lall, S., and F. Stewart. 1996. "Trade and Industrial Policy in Africa." In B. J. Ndulu and N. Van de Walle, ed., *Agenda for Africa's Economic Renewal*. Washington, D.C.: Overseas Development Institute.

Mbilinyi, M., ed. 1993. "Review of Women's Conditions and Positions in Tanzania: Issues and Methodology." Background paper prepared for the Tanzania Gender Networking Program. Unpublished.

Ministry of Health. 1997. "Adult Morbidity and Mortality Project Report." Dar es Salaam.

_____. 1999. "Adult Morbidity and Mortality Project Report." Dar es Salaam.

Muhimbili Medical Center and National AIDS Control Program. 1999. "Report on National Multisectoral AIDS Conference in Tanzania." Dar es Salaam.

Ndulu, B., and N. Van de Walle. 1996. "Overview: Africa's Economic Renewal: from Consensus to Strategy". In B. J. Ndulu and N. Van de Walle, eds., *Agenda for Africa's Economic Renewal*. Washington, D.C.: Overseas Development Institute.

Research on Poverty Alleviation. 1998. "Economic Policy Changes and Rural Poverty—Survey Data." Unpublished.

Sahn, D., D. Stifel, and S. Younger. 1999. *Intertemporal Changes in Welfare: Preliminary Results from Nine African Countries*. Ithaca, New York: Cornell University.

URT (United Republic of Tanzania). 1986. *Economic Recovery Programme (ERP)*. Dar es Salaam.

_____. 1993. *The Labor Force Survey 1990/91*. Dar es Salaam: Bureau of Statistics.

_____. 1996. *Human Resource Development Survey, 1996*. Dar es Salaam.

_____. 1998a. *The National Poverty Eradication Strategy*. Dar es Salaam: Government Printer.

_____. 1998b. *The Tanzania Vision 2025*. Dar es Salaam: Planning Commission.

_____. 1999a. "Consultation on Trade-Related Assistance." Report prepared by the Ministry of Commerce in consultation with other concerned ministries and private sector organizations. Draft.

_____. 1999b. "Report on Poverty and Welfare Monitoring Indicators." Vice President's Office, Dar es Salaam.

_____. 1999c. "Preparatory Workshop for Developing Tools for Home-Based Care Services in Tanzania," Ministry of Health, Dar es Salaam.

Wobst, P. 1999. "Structural Adjustment and Income Distribution in Tanzania: A Computable General Equilibrium (CGE) Analysis Using a 1992 Social Accounting Matrix (SAM)." Ph. D. diss., Institute for Agricultural Economics and Social Sciences in the Tropics and Subtropics, University of Hohenheim, Germany.

World Bank. 1992. *World Development Indicators*. Washington, D.C.

_____. 1993. *Tanzania: A Poverty Profile*. Washington, D.C.

_____. 1996. *Tanzania: The Challenge of Reforms: Growth, Incomes and Welfare Volume*. Washington, D.C.

_____. 1998. *Tanzania, Agriculture, and the World Bank*. Washington, D.C.

_____. 1999. *Tanzania Peri-Urban Study*. Washington, D.C.

_____. 2000. *Agriculture in Tanzania since 1986: Follower or Leader of Growth?* Washington, D.C.

World Economic Forum and Center for International Development. 2000. *The Africa Competitiveness Report 2000/2001*. Cambridge, Massachusetts: Harvard University.

Distributors of World Bank Group Publications

Prices and credit terms vary from country to country. Consult your local distributor before placing an order.

ARGENTINA
World Publications SA
Av. Cordoba 1877
1120 Ciudad de Buenos Aires
Tel: (54 11) 4815-8156
Fax: (54 11) 4815-8156
E-mail: wpbooks@infovia.com.ar

AUSTRALIA, FIJI, PAPUA NEW GUINEA, SOLOMON ISLANDS, VANUATU, AND SAMOA
D.A. Information Services
648 Whitehorse Road
Mitcham 3132, Victoria
Tel: (61) 3 9210 7777
Fax: (61) 3 9210 7788
E-mail: service@dadirect.com.au
URL: http://www.dadirect.com.au

AUSTRIA
Gerold and Co.
Weihburggasse 26
A-1011 Wien
Tel: (43 1) 512-47-31-0
Fax: (43 1) 512-47-31-29
URL: http://www.gerold.co/at.online

BANGLADESH
Micro Industries Development Assistance Society (MIDAS)
House 5, Road 16
Dhanmondi R/Area
Dhaka 1209
Tel: (880 2) 326427
Fax: (880 2) 811188

BELGIUM
Jean De Lannoy
Av. du Roi 202
1060 Brussels
Tel: (32 2) 538-5169
Fax: (32 2) 538-0841

BRAZIL
Publicacões Tecnicas Internacionais Ltda.
Rua Peixoto Gomide, 209
01409 Sao Paulo, SP.
Tel: (55 11) 259-6644
Fax: (55 11) 258-6990
E-mail: postmaster@pti.uol.br
URL: http://www.uol.br

CANADA
Renouf Publishing Co. Ltd.
5369 Canotek Road
Ottawa, Ontario K1J 9J3
Tel: (613) 745-2665
Fax: (613) 745-7660
E-mail: order.dept@renoufbooks.com
URL: http:// www.renoufbooks.com

CHINA
China Financial & Economic Publishing House
8, Da Fo Si Dong Jie
Beijing
Tel: (86 10) 6401-7365
Fax: (86 10) 6401-7365

China Book Import Centre
P.O. Box 2825
Beijing

Chinese Corporation for Promotion of Humanities
52, You Fang Hu Tong,
Xuan Nei Da Jie
Beijing
Tel: (86 10) 660 72 494
Fax: (86 10) 660 72 494

COLOMBIA
Infoenlace Ltda.
Carrera 6 No. 51-21
Apartado Aereo 34270
Santafé de Bogotá, D.C.
Tel: (57 1) 285-2798
Fax: (57 1) 285-2798

COTE D'IVOIRE
Center d'Edition et de Diffusion Africaines (CEDA)
04 B.P. 541
Abidjan 04
Tel: (225) 24 6510; 24 6511
Fax: (225) 25 0567

CYPRUS
Center for Applied Research
Cyprus College
6, Diogenes Street, Engomi
P.O. Box 2006
Nicosia
Tel: (357 2) 59-0730
Fax: (357 2) 66-2051

CZECH REPUBLIC
USIS, NIS Prodejna
Havelkova 22
130 00 Prague 3
Tel: (420 2) 2423 1486
Fax: (420 2) 2423 1114
URL: http://www.nis.cz/

DENMARK
SamfundsLitteratur
Rosenoerns Allé 11
DK-1970 Frederiksberg C
Tel: (45 35) 351942
Fax: (45 35) 357822
URL: http://www.sl.cbs.dk

ECUADOR
Libri Mundi
Libreria Internacional
P.O. Box 17-01-3029
Juan Leon Mera 851
Quito
Tel: (593 2) 521-606; (593 2) 544-185
Fax: (593 2) 504-209
E-mail: librimu1@librimundi.com.ec
E-mail: librimu2@librimundi.com.ec

CODEU
Ruiz de Castilla 763, Edif. Expocolor
Primer piso, Of. #2
Quito
Tel/Fax: (593 2) 507-383; 253-091
E-mail: codeu@impsat.net.ec

EGYPT, ARAB REPUBLIC OF
Al Ahram Distribution Agency
Al Galaa Street
Cairo
Tel: (20 2) 578-6083
Fax: (20 2) 578-6833

The Middle East Observer
41, Sherif Street
Cairo
Tel: (20 2) 393-9732
Fax: (20 2) 393-9732

FINLAND
Akateeminen Kirjakauppa
P.O. Box 128
FIN-00101 Helsinki
Tel: (358 0) 121 4418
Fax: (358 0) 121-4435
E-mail: akatilaus@stockmann.fi
URL: http://www.akateeminen.com

FRANCE
Editions Eska; DBJ
48, rue Gay Lussac
75005 Paris
Tel: (33-1) 55-42-73-08
Fax: (33-1) 43-29-91-67

GERMANY
UNO-Verlag
Poppelsdorfer Allee 55
53115 Bonn
Tel: (49 228) 949020
Fax: (49 228) 217492
URL: http://www.uno-verlag.de
E-mail: unoverlag@aol.com

GHANA
Epp Books Services
P.O. Box 44
TUC
Accra
Tel: 223 21 778843
Fax: 223 21 779099

GREECE
Papasotiriou S.A.
35, Stournara Str.
106 82 Athens
Tel: (30 1) 364-1826
Fax: (30 1) 364-8254

HAITI
Culture Diffusion
5, Rue Capois
C.P. 257
Port-au-Prince
Tel: (509) 23 9260
Fax: (509) 23 4858

HONG KONG, CHINA; MACAO
Asia 2000 Ltd.
Sales & Circulation Department
302 Seabird House
22-28 Wyndham Street, Central
Hong Kong, China
Tel: (852) 2530-1409
Fax: (852) 2526-1107
E-mail: sales@asia2000.com.hk
URL: http://www.asia2000.com.hk

HUNGARY
Euro Info Service
Margitszgeti Europa Haz
H-1138 Budapest
Tel: (36 1) 350 80 24, 350 80 25
Fax: (36 1) 350 90 32
E-mail: euroinfo@mail.matav.hu

INDIA
Allied Publishers Ltd.
751 Mount Road
Madras - 600 002
Tel: (91 44) 852-3938
Fax: (91 44) 852-0649

INDONESIA
Pt. Indira Limited
Jalan Borobudur 20
P.O. Box 181
Jakarta 10320
Tel: (62 21) 390-4290
Fax: (62 21) 390-4289

IRAN
Ketab Sara Co. Publishers
Khaled Eslamboli Ave., 6th Street
Delafrooz Alley No. 8
P.O. Box 15745-733
Tehran 15117
Tel: (98 21) 8717819; 8716104
Fax: (98 21) 8712479
E-mail: ketab-sara@neda.net.ir

Kowkab Publishers
P.O. Box 19575-511
Tehran
Tel: (98 21) 258-3723
Fax: (98 21) 258-3723

IRELAND
Government Supplies Agency
Oifig an tSoláthair
4-5 Harcourt Road
Dublin 2
Tel: (353 1) 661-3111
Fax: (353 1) 475-2670

ISRAEL
Yozmot Literature Ltd.
P.O. Box 56055
3 Yohanan Hasandlar Street
Tel Aviv 61560
Tel: (972 3) 5285-397
Fax: (972 3) 5285-397

R.O.Y. International
PO Box 13056
Tel Aviv 61130
Tel: (972 3) 649 9469
Fax: (972 3) 648 6039
E-mail: royil@netvision.net.il
URL: http://www.royint.co.il

Palestinian Authority/Middle East
Index Information Services
P.O.B. 19502 Jerusalem
Tel: (972 2) 6271219
Fax: (972 2) 6271634

ITALY, LIBERIA
Licosa Commissionaria Sansoni SPA
Via Duca Di Calabria, 1/1
Casella Postale 552
50125 Firenze
Tel: (39 55) 645-415
Fax: (39 55) 641-257
E-mail: licosa@ftbcc.it
URL: http://www.ftbcc.it/licosa

JAMAICA
Ian Randle Publishers Ltd.
206 Old Hope Road, Kingston 6
Tel: 876-927-2085
Fax: 876-977-0243
E-mail: irpl@colis.com

JAPAN
Eastern Book Service
3-13 Hongo 3-chome, Bunkyo-ku
Tokyo 113
Tel: (81 3) 3818-0861
Fax: (81 3) 3818-0864
E-mail: orders@svt-ebs.co.jp
URL: http://www.bekkoame.or.jp/~svt-ebs

KENYA
Africa Book Service (E.A.) Ltd.
Quaran House, Mfangano Street
P.O. Box 45245
Nairobi
Tel: (254 2) 223 641
Fax: (254 2) 330 272

Legacy Books
Loita House
Mezzanine 1
P.O. Box 68077
Nairobi
Tel: (254) 2-330853, 221426
Fax: (254) 2-330854, 561654
E-mail: Legacy@form-net.com

KOREA, REPUBLIC OF
Dayang Books Trading Co.
International Division
783-20, Pangba Bon-Dong,
Socho-ku
Seoul
Tel: (82 2) 536-9555
Fax: (82 2) 536-0025
E-mail: seamap@chollian.net

Eulyoo Publishing Co., Ltd.
46-1, Susong-Dong
Jongro-Gu
Seoul
Tel: (82 2) 734-3515
Fax: (82 2) 732-9154

LEBANON
Librairie du Liban
P.O. Box 11-9232
Beirut
Tel: (961 9) 217 944
Fax: (961 9) 217 434
E-mail: hsayegh@librairie-du-liban.com.lb
URL: http://www.librairie-du-liban.com.lb

MALAYSIA
University of Malaya Cooperative Bookshop, Limited
P.O. Box 1127
Jalan Pantai Baru
59700 Kuala Lumpur
Tel: (60 3) 756-5000
Fax: (60 3) 755-4424
E-mail: umkoop@tm.net.my

MEXICO
INFOTEC
Av. San Fernando No. 37
Col. Toriello Guerra
14050 Mexico, D.F.
Tel: (52 5) 624-2800
Fax: (52 5) 624-2822
E-mail: infotec@rtn.net.mx
URL: http://rtn.net.mx

Mundi-Prensa Mexico S.A. de C.V.
c/Rio Panuco, 141-Colonia Cuauhtemoc
06500 Mexico, D.F.
Tel: (52 5) 533-5658
Fax: (52 5) 514-6799

NEPAL
Everest Media International Services (P.) Ltd.
GPO Box 5443
Kathmandu
Tel: (977 1) 416 026
Fax: (977 1) 224 431

NETHERLANDS
De Lindeboom/Internationale Publicaties b.v.
P.O. Box 202, 7480 AE Haaksbergen
Tel: (31 53) 574-0004
Fax: (31 53) 572-9296
E-mail: lindeboo@worldonline.nl
URL: http://www.worldonline.nl/~lindeboo

NEW ZEALAND
EBSCO NZ Ltd.
Private Mail Bag 99914
New Market
Auckland
Tel: (64 9) 524-8119
Fax: (64 9) 524-8067

Oasis Official
P.O. Box 3627
Wellington
Tel: (64 4) 499 1551
Fax: (64 4) 499 1972
E-mail: oasis@actrix.gen.nz
URL: http://www.oasisbooks.co.nz/

NIGERIA
University Press Limited
Three Crowns Building Jericho
Private Mail Bag 5095
Ibadan
Tel: (234 22) 41-1356
Fax: (234 22) 41-2056

PAKISTAN
Mirza Book Agency
65, Shahrah-e-Quaid-e-Azam
Lahore 54000
Tel: (92 42) 735 3601
Fax: (92 42) 576 3714

Oxford University Press
5 Bangalore Town
Sharae Faisal
PO Box 13033
Karachi-75350
Tel: (92 21) 446307
Fax: (92 21) 4547640
E-mail: ouppak@TheOffice.net

Pak Book Corporation
Aziz Chambers 21, Queen's Road
Lahore
Tel: (92 42) 636 3222; 636 0885
Fax: (92 42) 636 2328
E-mail: pbc@brain.net.pk

PERU
Editorial Desarrollo SA
Apartado 3824, Ica 242 OF. 106
Lima 1
Tel: (51 14) 285380
Fax: (51 14) 286628

PHILIPPINES
International Booksource Center Inc.
1127-A Antipolo St, Barangay, Venezuela
Makati City
Tel: (63 2) 896 6501; 6505; 6507
Fax: (63 2) 896 1741

POLAND
International Publishing Service
Ul. Piekna 31/37
00-677 Warzawa
Tel: (48 2) 628-6089
Fax: (48 2) 621-7255
E-mail: books%ips@ikp.atm.com.pl
URL: http://www.ipscg.waw.pl/ips/export

PORTUGAL
Livraria Portugal
Apartado 2681, Rua Do Carm o 70-74
1200 Lisbon
Tel: (1) 347-4982
Fax: (1) 347-0264

ROMANIA
Compani De Librarii Bucuresti S.A.
Str. Lipscani no. 26, sector 3
Bucharest
Tel: (40 1) 313 9645
Fax: (40 1) 312 4000

RUSSIAN FEDERATION
Isdatelstvo <Ves Mir>
9a, Kolpachniy Pereulok
Moscow 101831
Tel: (7 095) 917 87 49
Fax: (7 095) 917 92 59
ozimarin@glasnet.ru

SINGAPORE; TAIWAN, CHINA MYANMAR; BRUNEI
Hemisphere Publication Services
41 Kallang Pudding Road #04-03
Golden Wheel Building
Singapore 349316
Tel: (65) 741-5166
Fax: (65) 742-9356
E-mail: ashgate@asianconnect.com

SLOVENIA
Gospodarski vestnik Publishing Group
Dunajska cesta 5
1000 Ljubljana
Tel: (386 61) 133 83 47; 132 12 30
Fax: (386 61) 133 80 30
E-mail: repansekj@gvestnik.si

SOUTH AFRICA, BOTSWANA
For single titles:
Oxford University Press Southern Africa
Vasco Boulevard, Goodwood
P.O. Box 12119, N1 City 7463
Cape Town
Tel: (27 21) 595 4400
Fax: (27 21) 595 4430
E-mail: oxford@oup.co.za

For subscription orders:
International Subscription Service
P.O. Box 41095
Craighall
Johannesburg 2024
Tel: (27 11) 880-1448
Fax: (27 11) 880-6248
E-mail: iss@is.co.za

SPAIN
Mundi-Prensa Libros, S.A.
Castello 37
28001 Madrid
Tel: (34 91) 4 363700
Fax: (34 91) 5 753998
E-mail: libreria@mundiprensa.es
URL: http://www.mundiprensa.com/

Mundi-Prensa Barcelona
Consell de Cent, 391
08009 Barcelona
Tel: (34 3) 488-3492
Fax: (34 3) 487-7659
E-mail: barcelona@mundiprensa.es

SRI LANKA, THE MALDIVES
Lake House Bookshop
100, Sir Chittampalam Gardiner Mawatha
Colombo 2
Tel: (94 1) 32105
Fax: (94 1) 432104
E-mail: LHL@sri.lanka.net

SWEDEN
Wennergren-Williams AB
P. O. Box 1305
S-171 25 Solna
Tel: (46 8) 705-97-50
Fax: (46 8) 27-00-71
E-mail: mail@wwi.se

SWITZERLAND
Librairie Payot Service Institutionnel
C(tm)tes-de-Montbenon 30
1002 Lausanne
Tel: (41 21) 341-3229
Fax: (41 21) 341-3235

ADECO Van Diermen EditionsTechniques
Ch. de Lacuez 41
CH1807 Blonay
Tel: (41 21) 943 2673
Fax: (41 21) 943 3605

THAILAND
Central Books Distribution
306 Silom Road
Bangkok 10500
Tel: (66 2) 2336930-9
Fax: (66 2) 237-8321

TRINIDAD & TOBAGO AND THE CARRIBBEAN
Systematics Studies Ltd.
St. Augustine Shopping Center
Eastern Main Road, St. Augustine
Trinidad & Tobago, West Indies
Tel: (868) 645-8466
Fax: (868) 645-8467
E-mail: tobe@trinidad.net

UGANDA
Gustro Ltd.
PO Box 9997, Madhvani Building
Plot 16/4 Jinja Rd.
Kampala
Tel: (256 41) 251 467
Fax: (256 41) 251 468
E-mail: gus@swiftuganda.com

UNITED KINGDOM
Microinfo Ltd.
P.O. Box 3, Omega Park, Alton,
Hampshire GU34 2PG
England
Tel: (44 1420) 86848
Fax: (44 1420) 89889
E-mail: wbank@microinfo.co.uk
URL: http://www.microinfo.co.uk

The Stationery Office
51 Nine Elms Lane
London SW8 5DR
Tel: (44 171) 873-8400
Fax: (44 171) 873-8242
URL: http://www.the-stationery-office.co.uk/

VENEZUELA
Tecni-Ciencia Libros, S.A.
Centro Cuidad Comercial Tamanco
Nivel C2, Caracas
Tel: (58 2) 959 5547; 5035; 0016
Fax: (58 2) 959 5636

ZAMBIA
University Bookshop, University of Zambia
Great East Road Campus
P.O. Box 32379
Lusaka
Tel: (260 1) 252 576
Fax: (260 1) 253 952

ZIMBABWE
Academic and Baobab Books (Pvt.) Ltd.
4 Conald Road, Graniteside
P.O. Box 567
Harare
Tel: 263 4 755035
Fax: 263 4 781913

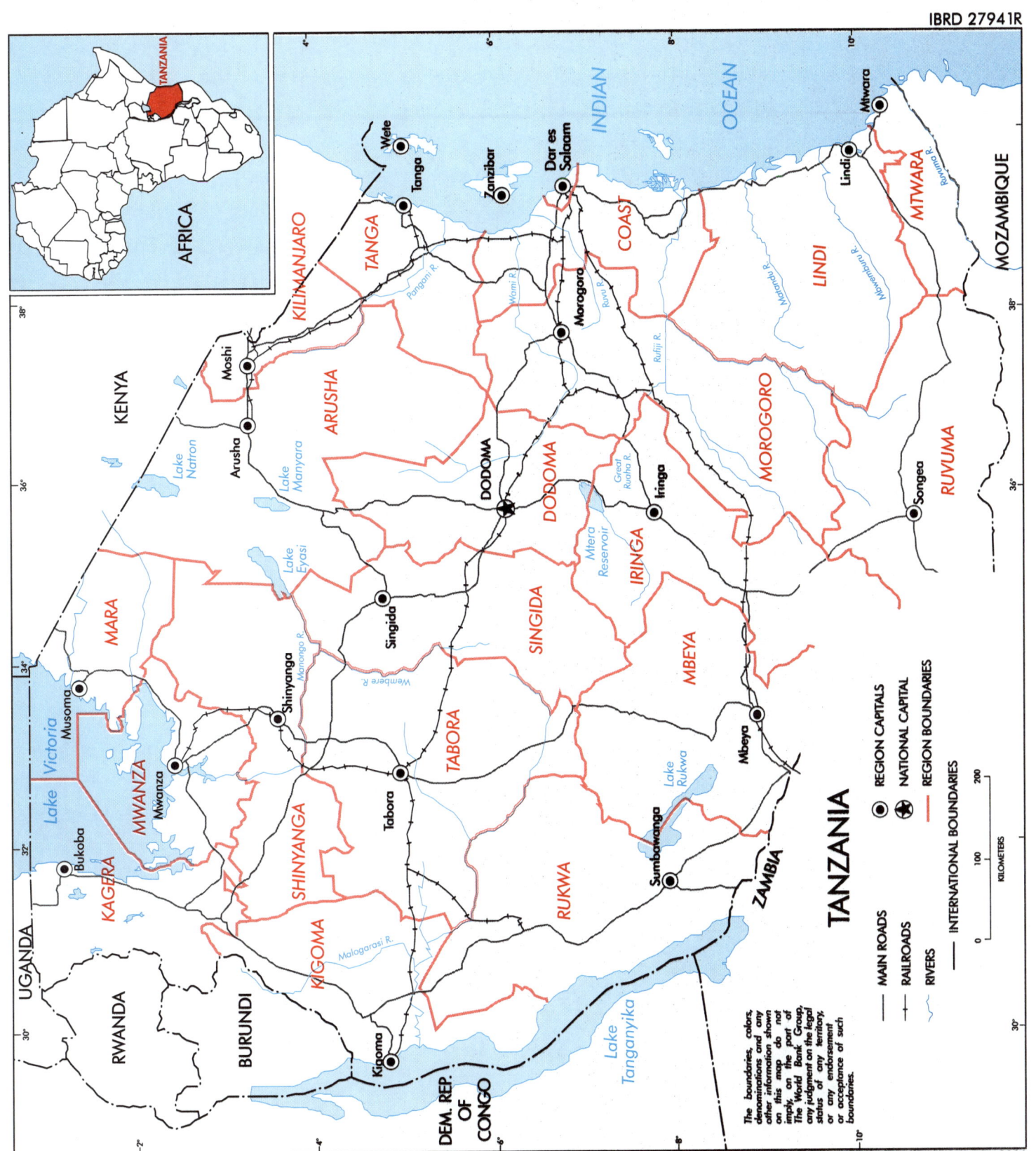

IBRD 27941R

AFRICA

TANZANIA

JULY 2000

INDIAN OCEAN

MOZAMBIQUE

KENYA

UGANDA

RWANDA

BURUNDI

DEM. REP. OF CONGO

ZAMBIA

KILIMANJARO

TANGA

ARUSHA

COAST

LINDI

MTWARA

MOROGORO

RUVUMA

MARA

DODOMA

SINGIDA

IRINGA

MBEYA

MWANZA

KAGERA

SHINYANGA

KIGOMA

TABORA

RUKWA

Mtwara

Lindi

Songea

Wete

Tanga

Zanzibar

Dar es Salaam

Moshi

Arusha

Morogora

DODOMA

Iringa

Singida

Shinyanga

Musoma

Bukoba

Mwanza

Tabora

Mbeya

Sumbawanga

Kigoma

Lake Natron

Lake Manyara

Lake Eyasi

Lake Victoria

Lake Tanganyika

Lake Rukwa

Mtera Reservoir

Pangani R.

Wami R.

Ruvu R.

Rufiji R.

Matandu R.

Mbemkuru R.

Ruvuma R.

Great Ruaha R.

Mbarangandu R.

Wembere R.

Manonga R.

Malagarasi R.

REGION CAPITALS
NATIONAL CAPITAL
REGION BOUNDARIES
MAIN ROADS
RAILROADS
RIVERS
INTERNATIONAL BOUNDARIES

0   100   200
KILOMETERS

The boundaries, colors, denominations and any other information shown on this map do not imply, on the part of The World Bank Group, any judgment on the legal status of any territory, or any endorsement or acceptance of such boundaries.